JUICING FOR BEGINNERS

COOKBOOK

600 Foolproof Juicing Recipes and the Complete Crash Course to Juicing to Lose Weight, Gain energy, Anti-age, Detox, Fight Disease, and Live Long

DAWN J. WASHINGTON

Table of Contents

Foreword

Congratulations on your decision to take a step in the direction of a healthier lifestyle by opting to implement juicing into your diet. Think of this book as your one stop resource to get started with juicing.

Whether you received a juicer over the holidays or you're are in the midst of a New Year's resolution kick, you may simply want to get more fresh fruits and vegetables in your diet, or you're just curious about juicing, whatever the case may be, shopping for a home juicer and finding juicing recipes that work for you can be daunting. But you do not need to be discouraged because making fresh fruit and vegetable juice at home can be very simple and fun when you have the right resources to guide you. It is on this note that we are thrilled to invite you to a life-altering journey, during which you will discover the true benefits that Mother Nature can offer us.

Getting this book is your first step to an exciting journey of providing yourself with a full-scale knowledge on juicing and an amazing collection of juicing recipes that will provide you with a healthy amount of vitamins, minerals, nutrients, and other microelements and at the same time shedding all your excess weight like you never had it.

Juicing is no miracle, magic, or professional cooking trick. It is simply the process of extracting or squeezing the juice from whole vegetables and fruit. It is also a method through which you can easily increase your daily intake of essential nutrients while also cleansing your body and boosting your weight-loss efforts. If you have ever struggled to lose weight, juicing may be the solution you've been looking for.

In this book, you will find a comprehensive overview of the benefits of juicing along with 600 juicing recipes to help you begin this delicious and healthy life choice. Not only will you learn the details of how juicing can improve your health and boost your weight loss, but you will learn exactly what nutritional benefits raw fruits and vegetables have to offer. Equipped with all of this valuable information and the recipes you need to get started; you will be ready to juice right away. We wish you a "juicy" journey ahead!

Introduction

Whether you're hoping to kick-start weight loss, feel more energised or get glowing skin, juicing can be a positive new habit that delivers a whole host of health benefits. The benefits of freshly juiced fruits and vegetables are amazing, the taste just can't be beaten, and with a new generation of juice machines, it's quicker, easier, and more affordable than ever before!

If you are new to juicing then you have a great treat in store. Not only are the health benefits of freshly extracted juices unbelievably good, but you'll be surprised how wonderful the flavours of juices can be. Even foods you never believed you would enjoy are suddenly transformed into succulent, rich-tasting super juices in a matter of seconds.

Juicing is a process that extracts the liquid from raw vegetables and fruits. This liquid – or juice – is bursting with minerals, antioxidants and vitamins, creating a delicious and nutritious drink. Each piece of fruit or veg that is juiced creates a pulp by-product, which is made up of the left-over skin, pips and fibrous material.

While the first juicing machine was developed around the 1950s, it didn't become popular until two decades later, spurred on by Dave Otto, who launched the first juice bar in California. Today, a whole new generation of juicers continue to keep the trend alive, with home juicing becoming favoured for its convenience, affordability and accessibility.

Juicing at home can create healthy habits for the whole family and also means you know exactly what you're consuming – unlike supermarket-bought juices that can be laden with shelf-lengthening preservatives and sugars.

This book is full of the information you'll need to make delicious fresh juices with confidence. This book covers what juicing is and how it differs from making smoothies. You'll also find a useful section on different types of juicing machines so that you'll know how to select one that is right for you. Finally, you'll learn about the steps to juicing and there are hundreds of nutritious recipes in this book to get you started.

Chapter 1
Juicing Basics

We are told all the time that we should try our best to include five fruit and vegetables into our daily diet. But as nice as that would be, in reality it can be time consuming and difficult to do so. Juicing however is one of the easiest ways to incorporate natures goodness back into your diet and requires very little preparation. But what exactly is juicing? Juicing is the process of squeezing juice out of vegetables and fruits, extracting all of the nutrients from the plant and removing the pulp to leave you with a pure and healthy drink.

More and more people are turning to fresh juice to improve their health. Numerous scientific studies show that diets rich in fruits and vegetables, such as the Mediterranean Diet, reduce the risk of developing many illnesses including diabetes, heart disease, and even cancer. Certain combinations of fruits and vegetables are now known to effectively treat certain diseases such as Type II diabetes. And that's not all. Juicing can even save you money. You can stop buying multivitamins and other nutritional supplements because fresh homemade juice gives you all your daily nutritional needs and more!

Even the best brand of bottled juice doesn't come close to delivering all the nutrients found in homemade juice, because any juice sold commercially must by law be heated – a process known as pasteurization – which kills many nutrients. Store it and you lose even more nutrients. Plus many juices add sugar, colors, stabilizers and other additives which also kill nutrients.

Reasons for Juicing

While the reasons for juicing might be significantly larger than the few listed here, the reasons below are perhaps some of the most convincing reasons behind the recent juicing trend.

PROCESSED VS. NATURAL JUICE

Fruit juices are widely available in grocery stores and supermarkets alike. This, however, does not mean that drinking store bought fruit juice is a better option than creating your own, and it also doesn't mean that you reap the same rewards. Processed juices such as the ones readily accessible at your local grocery store don't provide the same benefits that fresh and organic juices do, and are often stuffed to the brim with sugar or sugar substitutes that would never be present in a juice you create at home.

HEALTHY MEAL REPLACEMENT

If you're looking to diet, juicing could be your way to ditch all the strict commandments and pump your meals with important nutrients that you may be lacking in a regular dieting regimen. Instead of eating out at a fast food restaurant, you can reward your body with a juiced drink that contains an explosive variety of minerals and vitamins. You can also use these drinks in-between meals to keep you from feeling hungry as well as provide a supplement in potential nutrient-deprived food spreads.

ENCOURAGES HEALTHY EATING HABITS

Admittedly, not all vegetables and fruits are as tasty as you might want them to be. This barrier in consuming your proper share is easily destroyed with juicing. Juicing blends flavours in new and exciting ways, creating not only a fun new way to get your veggies down, but also a delicious one. This can be a huge boon when it comes to feeding more finicky eaters, especially with children. A juice blend becomes an exhilarating and refreshing experiment to share between parents and kids, all the while benefiting both physically.

Juicing Versus Blending

Juicing and blending are two easy ways to boost your daily intake of fruits and veggies. Both involve liquefying fruits or vegetables into smoothies or juices. Here's what you need to know about juicing and blending and how they can affect your health.

DIFFERENCES BETWEEN JUICING AND BLENDING

Doctors recommend eating at least five servings of fruits and vegetables each day, but studies show that people are averaging only about one serving per day. Because of this, juicing and blending have become popular options when it comes to getting more fruits and veggies.

As mentioned earlier, juicing is a way to consume fruits or vegetables in liquid form. You need a juicer, an appliance that separates the pulp (fiber) of the fruit or vegetable from the liquid. The liquid is thin and easy to drink, and it has the vitamins and minerals from the fruits and vegetables. You do not drink parts of the fruit like the peel or pulp. Blending is another way to get in several servings of fruits and vegetables by blending or making smoothies. You use the whole fruit or vegetable, sometimes including the skin. Blending keeps the fiber and nutrients that you would get if you ate the whole fruit or veggie.

When blending fruits or vegetables, you drink whatever it is that you put into your blender, as there is no separation of the pulp from the liquid. You need fewer fruits and veggies to make a smoothie than you would need to make a serving of juice, as you are using the whole product.

PROS OF JUICING AND BLENDING

Both juicing and blending smoothies can offer several health benefits, since they can help you fit in more servings of healthy fruits and veggies every day. Both can help fight against heart disease by lowering your blood pressure and bad cholesterol.

There are benefits to both juicing and blending. Each have their own place in a healthy diet. Smoothies are usually made with fruit suitable for a smoothie and a few servings of vegetables at most. Liquid is often added to the blender to help blend up the produce. Protein powders, nut butters, and seeds can be added for more nutrition. Smoothies are fast and convenient portable meals.

You won't find bananas, nut butters, or many other popular smoothie ingredients in a juice. Because the fiber is removed, a 16-ounce glass of juice can contain the nutrition of a dozen or more servings of produce. If you tried to blend a pound of carrots, an apple, and half a bunch of kale, the resulting drink would be totally unpalatable. But juice those ingredients and you get a smooth, delicious beverage rich in nutrients. Because no water or other liquid is added to juice, the nutrition density is about 2.5:1 compared to a smoothie.

Juicing Versus Raw Fruits and Vegetables

For many people, making use of a juicer is a quick and easy way to boost the daily intake of fruits and vegetables. While it is true that some of the fiber content of the raw fruits and vegetables is lost during juicing, there are many unique benefits that juicing provides over eating raw fruits and vegetables. These include:
Juicing is an excellent alternative if you do not normally like eating raw fruits and vegetables.
The results are delicious—you can even disguise the flavor of vegetables by combining them with your favorite fruits.
Juicing is a quick and easy process; the resulting juice can be taken with you for an on-the-go meal.
Adding some of the pulp to your pressed juice will help restore some of its fiber content.
Juicing does not require you to peel or chop the produce before using it (depending on the type of juicer you buy).
Homemade juices have a fresh-squeezed taste; store-bought juices simply can't compare.
Juicing is a great way to help your kids get the vitamins and minerals they need from fruits and vegetables.
Leftover pulp from juicing can be used in baked goods, such as muffins, or as a base for homemade stocks and broths.
Juicing is an economical way to make use of fruits and vegetables that are about to spoil.

Juicing for Health

Many juicing advocates will express that the benefits of juicing are far-reaching. It is thought to supply the body with a vast amount of vitamins, nutrients and phytonutrients that are easily absorbed by the body, allowing it to rest and heal, instead of using up precious energy on digestion. Below are some of the many benefits of juices:

GENERAL HEALTH

Just one glass of freshly pressed juice each day provides more nutrition than most people get all week! In a 2017 meta-analysis of 95 studies that included more than two million people, researchers concluded that 10 servings of fruits and vegetables per day are needed for maximum protection from health issues like heart disease, cardiovascular disease, stroke, type 2 diabetes, cancer, and premature death. That's about 1¾ pounds of produce. Unfortunately, most people in the United States eat less than a cup of fruit and only about 1½ cups of vegetables per day. Since one 16-ounce juice could easily contain two pounds of produce, juicing makes it easy to maximize the health benefits of fruits and vegetables.

BRAIN HEALTH

Micronutrients called polyphenols are found in many fruits and vegetables and have powerful antioxidant properties that can help protect against Alzheimer's disease and dementia. In a study of more than 1,800 people, drinking polyphenol-rich fruit and vegetable juices three or more times per week was associated with a substantially decreased risk of Alzheimer's disease. Furthermore, another study shows that quercetin, a type of polyphenol, can cross the blood-brain barrier and reduce brain cancer cells' ability to multiply.

CLEANSING AND DETOXIFYING

Detoxification occurs on a cellular level. Cruciferous vegetables are rich in sulfur compounds that the body converts to isothiocyanates (ITCs), and orange, yellow, and green vegetables are high in beneficial pigments called carotenoids. When you juice these vegetables, you drive enzyme production that will help your body excrete carcinogens and heavy metals. Additionally, when you drink juice instead of eating raw foods, your body remains in a fasting state and can focus more energy on toxin removal.

DIGESTION

According to a recent survey by the National Institute of Diabetes and Digestive and Kidney Diseases, 60 to 70 million Americans are living with digestive complaints, such as gas, bloating, and abdominal pain. Juicing can help! Certain fruits and vegetables are especially useful to relieve constipation and bloating, reduce acid reflux, lower inflammation, and soothe irritated bowels. Drinking freshly pressed juice can even help rebuild intestinal walls and repair a leaky gut.

HEART HEALTH (OR CARDIOVASCULAR HEALTH)

Research proves that juicing can help you reduce your LDL cholesterol and triglycerides and raise beneficial HDL. The phytonutrients in fresh juice promote cardiovascular health by providing powerful antioxidants and anti-inflammatory nutrients to prevent the oxidation of LDL and help reduce the damage it causes. Juices can also help lower blood pressure naturally, an important factor in heart health.

IMMUNE SYSTEM

Fresh juice provides your body with energy, as well as the vitamins and micronutrients essential for healthy immune function, such as zinc, selenium, iron, copper, folate, and vitamins A, B6, C, and E. A single 16-ounce juice combination of carrot, yellow bell pepper, and parsley delivers more than twice the daily recommended amounts of vitamins A and C, as well as a substantial amount of vitamin B6, which plays a vital role in immune cell proliferation and antibody production.

BLOOD AND BONE HEALTH

Calcium, iron, zinc, manganese, folate, boron, and vitamins B6, B9, B12, and K are just a few of the nutrients necessary for building strong bones and healthy blood. Fortunately, these are found in abundance—and in an easy-to-assimilate form—in fresh juices, especially greens. Adding broccoli, Brussels sprouts, collards, kale, mustard greens, Swiss chard, and other greens to your juice blends provides calcium that is easy to absorb.

MENTAL HEALTH

Fresh juices can ease the symptoms of depression and help lift your mood and energy. Juices provide a quick and healthy energy boost, which can help you feel like doing more. Certain juice combinations can deliver high amounts of folate and vitamins C and K, which have been shown to help alleviate depression.
Juicing for Weight Loss

There are many reasons why juicing is helpful in promoting weight loss. For one thing, replacing typical meals of processed or fast foods with freshly squeezed juice will not only provide an increase in nutrient content, but it will also offer a significant reduction in calories. The basic science of weight loss is this: if you burn more calories than you consume, you will lose weight. This doesn't mean that you have to spend two hours on the treadmill every day just to burn off the food you eat.

As part of a healthy diet, juicing may help you lose weight by encouraging the flushing of excess toxins from your body, by increasing your nutrient intake, and by helping you create a calorie deficit. When you replace unhealthy, toxin-laden foods with nutrient-packed juices, you can start to restore the healthy function of your organs. Once your body is no longer being overloaded with incoming toxins, it can begin to rid itself of stored toxins. All of the nutrients in freshly pressed juices will boost your immune system and improve your organ function and overall health.

Chapter 2
Getting Started with Juicing

Knowing how to mix up your own combos of fruits and vegetables is an art that you will be able to master once you have learned the general formula for juicing. If you're new to juicing, this chapter will help answer some of the questions you may have about making juices

As you read on, you will learn everything you need to know to get started, from choosing the best juicing machine to how to create your very own juice. By the end, you should be able to avoid some of the common mistakes that prevent most people from becoming successful juicers!

Best Juicers for Beginners

Choosing a juicer can be a confusing process if you don't already understand the basics. Before you go shopping for your new juicer, take the time to learn about the three different types so you can decide which option is best for you. The three main types of juicers are: centrifugal juicers, masticating juicers, and triturating juicers. Each type has its own list of pros and cons, so in order to select the right one for your situation, you need to think about what features you want. You should also decide what price range you are willing to consider, because juicers can be quite expensive.

CENTRIFUGAL JUICERS

A centrifugal juicer is perhaps the simplest type of juicer. For one thing, it is easy to operate and easy to clean. Also, these juicers utilize a grated basket that acts as a spinning blade, grinding the produce and extracting the juice. The pulp remains in the basket while the juice passes through the holes and exits the appliance through the spout. These juicers work very quickly and are one of the most affordable options, but they are not well equipped to handle very hard produce or pitted fruits.

MASTICATING JUICERS

A masticating juicer operates more slowly than a centrifugal juicer. These juicers work by kneading and grinding the material in the feed chute, squeezing the juice out into a container. The benefit of this type of juicer is that it operates at a lower speed than other juicers, which means that it produces less heat. Because the juicer doesn't get very hot, fewer enzymes are killed, so the juice should not oxidize very much, giving it a longer shelf life.

TRITURATING JUICERS

A triturating juicer is a twin-gear juicer that utilizes a two-step juicing process. When produce is fed through the juicer, it is first crushed and then it is pressed. These appliances may be a little pricier, but they are the most efficient. They also produce little heat, which is ideal for preserving enzymes and limiting oxidization.

Fruit and Vegetables for Juicing

The following fruits and vegetables are the most popular choices for juicing. The nutrients and health benefits that have been discovered for each one could fill pages, and research is ongoing. But here are the most notable highlights that you may find interesting and helpful as you explore your juicing options.

FRUITS

Fresh, raw fruit juice is not only delicious, but it also contains vitamins, minerals, soluble fiber, and important disease-fighting phytonutrients. In a meta-analysis of 18 randomized controlled trials, consumption of 100 percent fruit juice was not associated with an increased risk of type 2 diabetes and did not negatively affect glycemic control. You can use fruit to sweeten and bring variety to your daily vegetable juice blends and enjoy 100 percent fruit juices on occasion if your health condition allows.

APPLES

Containing dozens of phytonutrients, apples provide antioxidants that protect blood vessels and the heart by reducing LDL cholesterol oxidation, which causes hardening of the arteries. Apples may also help lower total cholesterol and triglycerides. Pectin, the primary soluble fiber in apples, slows stomach emptying and helps stabilize blood sugar. Apples are also being researched for colon cancer prevention.

BLACKBERRIES

Blackberries are high in vitamin C and anthocyanins, which are important antioxidants that protect against cancer and heart disease. Blackberries are also a good source of vitamin K for proper blood clotting. In an animal study, blackberries improved cognitive function. Like most berries, blackberries are very low in sugar.

BLUEBERRIES

Like blackberries, blueberries are best known for their anthocyanins, which not only offer protection against heart disease and cancer but also boost cognitive function and memory. These powerhouse berries may also help regulate blood pressure and blood sugar. Stilbenoids, naturally occurring compounds found in blueberries, are chemoprotective, and lab studies show blueberry extracts inhibit cancer cell proliferation and induce apoptosis, or cancer cell death.

CANTALOUPE

Cantaloupe is an excellent source of vitamin C and vitamin A, which provides anti-inflammatory and antioxidant benefits. Cantaloupe is also a good source of B vitamins, vitamin K, and several minerals including copper, magnesium, and potassium. If the melon is organic, you can juice the rind.

CRANBERRIES

Packed full of outstanding phytonutrients, cranberry juice has been shown to raise HDL cholesterol, lower triglycerides, and reduce LDL cholesterol oxidation, lowering the risk of cardiovascular disease. This tart berry juice also lowers fasting blood sugar levels and helps increase levels of a hormone that decreases insulin resistance and fat storage. It may also help prevent or improve certain urinary tract infections.

DRAGON FRUIT (PITAYA, PITAHAYA)

This exotic-looking tropical fruit supplies vitamins, minerals, and fiber to your diet. Dragon fruit can help boost your iron levels and strengthen your immune system. The red variety contains betalains and carotenoids that are cancer protective. You can juice the thick outer skin along with the pulp and seeds.

GRAPEFRUIT

Grapefruit juice is highly antioxidant and offers a host of health benefits. High in vitamin C, it is anti-inflammatory, helps fight colds, and can reduce the severity of asthma and arthritis. Lycopene, found in red and pink grapefruit, and other phytonutrients in this citrus fruit are anticancer. This juice can also lower LDL cholesterol and may help prevent kidney stones. Include the inner white pith where the anti-inflammatory and antioxidant flavonoid hesperidin is found. (Avoid grapefruit if you are taking certain statin drugs, antimicrobials, blood thinners, pain medications, or certain other medications for blood pressure, heart rhythm, or prostate issues. Check your package insert or the **Drugs.com** "Drug Interactions Checker" page at **drugs. com/drug_interactions.html** for more information on food interactions.)

GRAPES

Grape juice is anticancer, antimicrobial, anti-inflammatory, and anti-aging. The cardiovascular benefits of grapes are lengthy, including reduced LDL, better blood pressure regulation, and reduced clumping of platelets. Grapes help balance blood sugar and increase insulin sensitivity. Grape juice is also good for your brain. Look for organic red, black, or purple grapes. Grapes with seeds are even better!

HONEYDEW MELON

Like cantaloupe, honeydew melon is a good source of vitamin C, which is important for collagen production and a healthy immune system. Honeydew's high potassium content can help prevent hypertension and supports healthy bones. With vitamin B6 and folate, honeydew helps support healthy brain function.

KIWIFRUIT

Kiwifruit is an excellent source of vitamin C. The phytonutrients in kiwifruit protect DNA from damage, and kiwi can lower your risk of blood clots without the side effects of aspirin. Kiwifruit consumption can also lower triglycerides. Juice the whole fruit; peeling is not necessary.

LEMONS

Like other citrus fruits, lemons are high in vitamin C, which helps fight free radicals. Lemons and limes contain important cancer-fighting compounds called limonoids that persist in the bloodstream many times longer than the anticancer compounds in green tea. Lemons are an important part of an anti-inflammatory diet. If your lemons are organic, juice them with their peels, which is where limonene and other beneficial flavonoids are found.

LIMES

Limes are very similar to lemons in nutrition and health benefits but are slightly more acidic. The flavonol glycoside found in limes has been shown to have antibiotic effects. Although you can juice lime peels, many people find them too bitter, so you may want to peel them.

MANGO

Mango is an excellent source of vitamin B6 and a good source of vitamins A and C. High in the soluble fiber pectin, mangos can help lower cholesterol and regulate digestion. Mango peel contains a unique antioxidant called mangiferin, which has been shown in animal studies to be anticancer and supports a healthy heart by lowering cholesterol and triglycerides.

ORANGES AND TANGERINES

Fresh orange juice is rich in vitamin C and a good source of folate, potassium, and magnesium. Orange juice consumption has been shown to lower cholesterol and blood pressure and decrease inflammation, and it may reduce the risk of kidney stones. Include the inner white pith where the anti-inflammatory and antioxidant flavonoid hesperidin is found.

PAPAYA

Heart-healthy papayas contain whopping amounts of vitamin C that can help boost your immunity and reduce stress hormones. They are also rich in vitamin A for eye health. Papaya contains the unique enzymes papain and chymopapain, which help reduce inflammation, improve digestion of proteins, and even relieve menstrual pain.

PASSION FRUIT

Fragrant, sweet, and tart passion fruit juice provides vitamins A and C, supporting your body's muscles, cartilage, blood vessels and collagen. It also supplies some iron, potassium, calcium, magnesium, and folate. Cut open this tropical fruit and scoop out the seeds and yellow flesh. Discard the peel.

Peaches and Nectarines

Peaches and nectarines are good sources of vitamins A and C, which are great for immunity and skin health. These stone fruits may reduce LDL, or "bad," cholesterol and help regulate blood pressure. Compounds in peaches and nectarines may improve skin hydration, reduce allergy symptoms, and even kill cancerous cells. Select firm, ripe peaches or nectarines for the most antioxidant activity.

PEARS

The flavonols in pears help improve insulin sensitivity. In studies, the phytonutrients in pears have been shown to reduce the risk of certain cancers, including gastric and esophageal cancers. Pears improve digestion and are considered a low-allergy food. Red pears contain anthocyanins in their skins and are good for heart health.

PINEAPPLE

Packed with vitamin C and manganese, pineapple juice is highly antioxidant and supports energy production in cells. Bromelain, found in the core, is a unique mixture of nutrients that is anti-inflammatory, improving osteoarthritis and reducing pain and swelling after surgery and strenuous exercise. Bromelain also improves digestion and has been shown in studies to be potentially anticancer.

PLUMS

Plums contain unique phenols that neutralize a particularly dangerous free radical that can damage healthy cells. They also prevent oxygen damage to fats, including brain cells. Plum juice contains soluble fiber that helps lower cholesterol and promote the growth of healthy bacteria in the gut.

POMEGRANATE

The juice of the ruby red arils inside a pomegranate has been shown to lower systolic blood pressure by about five points. It may also help keep carotid arteries clear and improve blood flow to the heart. This juice can help you maintain a healthy weight and may slow the progression of prostate cancer. Never juice the root, stem, or peel of a pomegranate because they contain poisons.

POMELO (PUMMELO)

Pomelo juice is nutritionally similar to grapefruit but isn't as tart. It's high in vitamin C, with one fruit supplying 600 percent of the recommended daily amount. It also supplies 37 percent of your daily potassium needs for good blood circulation. Include the inner white pith where the anti-inflammatory and antioxidant flavonoid hesperidin is found.

RASPBERRIES

This berry supplies high amounts of vitamin C, manganese, and fiber. Raspberries contain anthocyanins, which can help improve insulin and blood sugar balance. Raspberries are also anticancer and good for the brain. Look for ripe, organic berries for the greatest antioxidant benefits.

STRAWBERRIES

This popular berry can help regulate insulin and balance blood sugar. Strawberry intake is associated with delaying cognitive decline in older adults by up to 2½ years. Because they are very high in vitamin C and other antioxidants, strawberries are anticancer, anti-inflammatory, and good for heart health.

WATERMELON

Watermelon has more lycopene than tomatoes and is more easily absorbed. Watermelon is good for your heart and produces nitric oxide to fuel your performance in endurance sports. Researchers have found that watermelon juice can lower your risk of high blood pressure. Watermelon is also anti-inflammatory and antioxidant. The seeds are highly nutritious.

VEGETABLES

While many people find it easy to eat fruit, they may not be eating enough vegetables. Fortunately, vegetable juices deliver mind-blowing amounts of nutrition in just a few sips. Juicing dark leafy greens, as well as cruciferous and root vegetables, is without a doubt one of the best ways to ensure a healthy life. I encourage you to make daily vegetable-heavy juices the cornerstone of your healthy eating habits.

ARUGULA

This leafy green belongs to the cancer-fighting brassica family that includes broccoli and cabbage. Arugula is high in minerals, making it a good choice for bone health. This slightly bitter or peppery-tasting green supports detoxification and is best juiced along with other greens and vegetables.

ASPARAGUS

Asparagus is an excellent source of vitamins B1, B2, C, E, and K, as well as many minerals including folate, copper, and selenium. Asparagus is an important source of quercetin, a well-studied polyphenol that supports brain and cardiovascular health. This vegetable also contains common plant-based compounds called saponins that are anticancer. Asparagus is a natural diuretic and could irritate the kidneys in large amounts.

BEETS

Beets are powerful cleansers and should be used moderately in combination with other fruits and vegetables. Both red and gold beets are detoxifying and blood building. Beets are rich in nitrates, which your body converts to nitric oxide, improving blood flow and boosting stamina.

BELL PEPPERS

Red, yellow, and orange bell peppers are the best vegetable sources of vitamin C and good sources of a wide range of other vitamins and minerals for heart health, weight management, and balanced blood sugar. They're also high in carotenoids that support eye, brain, and heart health.

BOK CHOY

This cruciferous, cancer-fighting vegetable is easy on the palate and an excellent choice for juicing because its crunchy white or light green stalks are high in water. It contains more than 70 antioxidants, and it is anticancer and a good source of anti-inflammatory omega-3 fatty acids and vitamin K for blood and bone health.

BROCCOLI

Like other cruciferous vegetables, this highly studied anticancer food is anti-inflammatory and enhances detoxification. Some of its beneficial nutrients are damaged by heat, making it a good choice for juicing. Broccoli consumption is associated with lower LDL cholesterol, and it contains the antioxidants lutein and zeaxanthin for eye health.

CABBAGE

Cabbage is anti-inflammatory and anticancer. Cabbage juice can help prevent and heal peptic ulcers and can help relieve ulcerative colitis symptoms. Red or purple cabbage provides anthocyanins for heart health and red blood cell protection, as well as polyphenols that promote brain health.

CARROTS

In a large-scale 10-year study, carrots were associated with significantly lower cardiovascular disease risk. Carrots contain falcarinol, which is anticancer. Studies also support carrots for eye health and liver health. Beta-carotene, the most prominent antioxidant in carrots, helps boost immunity and is beneficial to overall good health. Red and purple carrots provide anthocyanins.

CAULIFLOWER

This white cruciferous vegetable is surprisingly high in vitamin C. Cauliflower and other cruciferous vegetables aid detoxification and support the body's immune, cardiovascular, and digestive systems. Cauliflower is also highly antioxidant.

CELERY

Celery juice contains antioxidant and anti-inflammatory nutrients that support the lining of the stomach and decrease the risk of gastric ulcers. Celery also contains powerful anticancer compounds. Celery provides vitamins, natural electrolytes, phenolic compounds, and other nutrients. You don't have to drink it plain to gain the benefits.

COLLARDS

Collard greens are a cruciferous vegetable offering cancer protection benefits due to their sulfur-containing compounds called glucosinolates. Collards also support cardiovascular health and a healthy digestive tract. This juice is strong-tasting, and one small leaf is enough to include in a juice to get the benefits.

CUCUMBERS

This high-volume juicing vegetable contains at least 73 different compounds that provide antioxidant and anti-inflammatory support. Polyphenols called lignans in cucumbers decrease the risk of estrogen-related cancers. Cucumber juice is also great for the skin.

DANDELION

Dandelion greens are full of vitamin K for bone and brain health. This often-overlooked herb is also a good source of vitamin A for healthy skin and eyes. Dandelion is high in soluble fiber to support heart health, weight management, and healthy gut flora. It also has a protective effect on the liver.

FENNEL

Slightly sweet fennel juice contains a unique array of phytonutrients, including a compound called anethole that is anti-inflammatory and anticancer. Fennel is also a good source of vitamin C, folate, and minerals.

KALE

Kale juice has been proven to lower LDL cholesterol, raise beneficial HDL cholesterol, and improve other cardiovascular health markers. This anti-inflammatory, antioxidant-rich, cruciferous leafy green helps with detoxification and cancer prevention. It's also the top lutein-containing food for eye health and the top source of vitamin K for healthy bones and blood.

KOHLRABI

This brassica family vegetable, related to cabbage, is anticancer and has more vitamin C than an orange. Kohlrabi is good for your overall health and promotes strong bones, a healthy weight, and good vision, digestion, and blood pressure. Kohlrabi juice has a strong flavor, so it's best to combine it with other vegetables.

MUSTARD GREENS

Pungent mustard greens are in the cruciferous family and provide anticancer, anti-inflammatory, and detoxification support. These greens are from the mustard plant, so their juice is warming and can improve circulation and relieve congestion. Mustard greens are a good source of vitamins K, A, and E, as well as calcium and iron. Start with one small leaf in a juice blend.

RADISH

Radish juice is high in vitamin C and is a good source of vitamin B6, potassium, folate, iron, and minerals. Radishes are traditionally used to treat asthma, jaundice, inflammation in the bladder, and kidney stones. They're also used as a diuretic, laxative, and blood purifier. Radishes are from the cruciferous family, and their sulfur compounds are anticancer and support detoxification.

ROMAINE

This lettuce is high in nutrition as well as water, making it an excellent choice for juice. Romaine provides vitamin C and beta-carotene to help prevent LDL oxidation. Its potassium and folic acid also support cardiovascular health. Look for large, heavy heads of romaine with dark outer leaves.

SPINACH

Spinach is the vegetable richest in chlorophyll, which helps delay stomach emptying, decrease hunger hormones, and increase satiety hormones, making it an excellent choice for weight loss or maintenance. Spinach is also an outstanding source of magnesium, iron, calcium, folate, and other vitamins.

SWEET POTATO

The proteins in sweet potatoes have been shown to suppress the growth of leukemia cells and colon cancer cells in a petri dish. Sweet potatoes are anti-inflammatory. They benefit the brain and nerves and help regulate blood sugar.

SWISS CHARD

Chard is high in vitamins K, A, and C. It is an excellent source of minerals and a good source of calcium. This leafy green is good for blood sugar regulation due to its array of B vitamins. Chard is good for cardiovascular health as it can help regulate blood pressure and reduce total and LDL cholesterol. Chard with colored stems provides anticancer and neuroprotective properties.

TOMATO

Containing lycopene and other antioxidants, tomatoes are best known for their cardiovascular benefits, including the ability to lower cholesterol and triglycerides and reduce the damage to healthy fats in the bloodstream. Tomatoes help lower the risk of prostate cancer in men and may reduce the risk of nonmelanoma skin cancer.

WINTER SQUASH

The orange flesh of most winter squash, like butternut and pumpkin, provide an array of anti-inflammatory carotenoids. Winter squash is also high in pectin, which helps regulate blood sugar and helps you feel fuller longer. This food group boosts your intake of almost every major category of nutrients.

ZUCCHINI

Summer squash like zucchini are good sources of minerals and B vitamins. Zucchini juice is cooling to the body and a natural colon cleanser. The flavor is bland, making it a good addition to juice blends with carrots or stronger-tasting greens.

HERBS, SPICES, AND MIX-INS

Apple Cider Vinegar

Organic, unfiltered apple cider vinegar has been proven to reduce fasting blood sugar better than antidiabetic drugs and to reduce blood sugar spikes from high glycemic meals by 23 percent. Vinegar has also been shown to support weight loss. Adding a couple of teaspoons to your juice can help you get to the optimal daily dose of two tablespoons, spread throughout the day.

CHIA SEEDS

Chia seeds are an excellent source of omega-3 fatty acids and a good source of plant protein, fiber, minerals, and antioxidants. When added to juice or water, the seeds swell and form a gel. Adding chia seeds to your juice will slow the rate of absorption and slow down detoxification on a juice fast if needed. They may also help improve satiety and reduce the number of calories you consume at a future meal.

CILANTRO

This leafy green herb is regarded as a detoxifier, helping your cells release heavy metals. When combined with a chelator like the algae chlorella, your body can more efficiently expel those metal toxins. Cilantro is also antibacterial, anti-inflammatory, and antidiabetic. It may help lower blood sugar, lower LDL cholesterol, and increase good HDL cholesterol. Limit cilantro juice to one ounce mixed into a juice blend.

CINNAMON

This warming and pleasant spice is anti-inflammatory, antibacterial, and antimicrobial. Cinnamon slows the rate of stomach emptying, reduces blood sugar spikes, and improves insulin sensitivity. The scent of this spice boosts brain activity. Ground cinnamon is especially tasty in apple, winter squash, and root vegetable juices.

COCONUT WATER

Coconut water from fresh, young Thai coconuts is a delicious tropical addition to your juices. Coconut water is hydrating, provides electrolytes and potassium, and cleanses the digestive tract. In animal studies, coconut water improved blood sugar control and lowered cholesterol.

GARLIC

Garlic is a natural antibiotic and is useful during cold and flu season to combat infections, expel phlegm, and alleviate congestion in the sinuses and lungs. Garlic is also anticancer and good for heart health. Juice the garlic first and follow with other vegetables, especially greens, to help remove the odor and flavor from your machine.

GINGER ROOT

Spicy and warming ginger juice is an effective expectorant, immunity booster, and digestive aid. It can relieve nausea, dizziness, and vomiting. Ginger is a powerful anti-inflammatory juice ingredient, relieving pain and swelling associated with osteoarthritis and rheumatoid arthritis. It is anticancer according to studies on gastrointestinal and ovarian cancer cells. Start with a ½- to 1-inch piece. You do not need to peel it.

PARSLEY

The juice of this herb is highly beneficial for the thyroid, adrenals, eyes, and urinary tract. It strengthens and cleanses the bladder and kidneys. Like cilantro, parsley helps your body get rid of heavy metals and chemical toxins. It's good for upper respiratory congestion and infections. Because parsley is so strong, never drink it alone in amounts greater than an ounce or two. Preferably, drink it in a juice blend.

SUPERFOOD POWDERS

Green superfood powders include algae, like spirulina and chlorella, and dehydrated grass juices, like wheatgrass, alfalfa, and barley. Berry superfood powders include acai, goji, camu camu, and maqui. These powders make it easy to boost your juice to the next level by adding highly antioxidant and phytonutrient-rich foods that are difficult or impossible to juice with a home machine. Read the ingredient lists and choose an organic brand without added sweeteners or fillers.

TURMERIC ROOT

The research on turmeric proves it to be anti-inflammatory, detoxifying, anticancer, blood sugar balancing, brain boosting, and heart healthy. The pigments in turmeric will permanently stain, so do not let turmeric juice sit on your countertop. Juice a 1-inch piece first and follow with the rest of your ingredients to help remove the staining oils from your machine. Add a pinch of black pepper to your turmeric juice blends to increase the absorption of curcumin, the main active compound in turmeric.

Produce Procedure

The quality of your juice depends on the quality of your produce. Certified organic or biodynamically grown fruits and vegetables are best. The age of your produce, how it's been stored, and how you prep your produce for juicing will influence the overall healthiness and nutritional value of your juice.

BUYING YOUR PRODUCE

Fruits and vegetables harvested at or close to their peak ripeness will have the most flavor and nutrition. Most grocery stores have a mix of produce grown nearby or in the region, as well as produce trucked in from across the country or shipped in from around the world. To maximize nutrition and flavor and reduce cost, make good use of locally grown or seasonal produce. If you have the space available, growing your own greens allows you to pick and juice immediately.

Also consider when you will be making juice and buy fruits and vegetables that will be in good condition by the time you are turning on your juicer. Limp greens don't make good juice! Plan out your juices and buy just enough produce to prevent waste.

WASHING YOUR PRODUCE

It's important to wash your produce properly to remove dirt and bacteria and reduce pesticide residues. Washing produce under running water and rubbing with your hand or a vegetable brush removes 98 percent of bacteria and 80 percent of pesticide residues. The water temperature should be as close to that of the produce you are washing as possible. If you prefer to use a vinegar-water solution, the effective formula is 1 part vinegar to 3 parts water. If you want to take a step further to remove more of the possible pesticides, you can soak hard produce in a sink filled with cold water and 4 tablespoons of baking soda (or a salad spinner–size bowl filled with water and 1 teaspoon of baking soda) for 5 to 15 minutes. After your vegetables have had their "bath," rinse them under running water, giving them a scrub. For leafy greens, a shorter soak time of 1 to 2 minutes followed by a rinse under running water will be enough. Delicate berries can be rinsed quickly with the baking soda water, then rinsed again under clean running water.

PREPPING YOUR PRODUCE

Before juicing, trim off the ends of root vegetables like carrots and beets because these areas can harbor bacteria. Always remove the very outer colored part of the rind of oranges, grapefruits, and mandarins. The volatile oils in these rinds are difficult to digest. Retain as much of the white pith as possible because this area contains valuable nutrients. You can leave on the rinds of lemons and limes, although some people find lime rinds very bitter. Peeling red beets can reduce their earthy flavor and make the juice more palatable but isn't required. Remove any limp leaves and any damaged areas or bad spots on your produce.

Basic Steps to Juicing

While the process of juicing is as easy as feeding fresh fruits and vegetables through your juicer, following the above steps will prepare you better for juicing. Preparations may vary depending on the type of juicer. When you are fully prepared, you can follow the steps below to start your juicing process:
Set up your juicer, ensuring all parts are assembled and fitted correctly and it's ready to go.

Choose the fruit and/or vegetables that you want to juice. Make sure all items are ripe with no nasty rotten or bruised areas.

Wash your produce by rinsing it under clean running water. Most items will just need a gentle rub with your hands, but certain items — like carrots or root veggies — might need a scrub with a vegetable brush.

Peel any items with thick skin or rind. While most juicers can handle thin skins on items like apples and pears, you'll need to remove thick skins on things like pineapple, bananas, citrus fruit, and melons.

Remove larger pits that can be found in cherries, peaches, plums etc.

Depending on the capacity and size of the feeder tube on your juicer, you may need to chop up some or all of your produce. Refer to your instruction manual and chop accordingly. Many models can handle whole apples, carrots, and beets. Once your produce is ready to go, turn the juicer on and begin inserting items into the feeding tube. Most models will have foolproof safety features, but make sure you never insert your hands or fingers into the tube.

Don't forget to adjust the speed setting — if your juicer has one — to account for different produce densities. Refer to your instruction manual.

If appropriate for your model, use the provided "pushing implement" to gently force the item down into the juicer. It may be helpful to vary the densities of produce as you go. Often, following a softer fruit like a kiwi or peach with a hard item like a carrot can assist in pushing the item through the juicer.

Once you are done juicing, give the juice a stir to blend the different flavors together.
Enjoy as soon as possible to get the most nutritional value from your tasty juice!
Clean your juicer as soon as possible to make the job easier and avoid any pulp or juice residue from sticking.

STORING YOUR JUICE
Juice made in a centrifugal juicer should be consumed immediately, or at least very soon after juicing. Centrifugal juicers whip air into the juice, speeding oxidation and the breakdown of beneficial phytonutrients.
Juice made in a masticating or a triturating juicer can generally be safely stored for 24 to 48 hours. Depending on your juicer and juicing conditions, you may be able to store a juice for up to 72 hours. Check with the manufacturer for its recommendations.
Fresh is best, but if you must store your juice, follow these guidelines:
Oxygen is the enemy. You can use canning jars with a lid and a screw band and either fill the jar to the rim or use a vacuum sealer to remove the air.
Store your juice in the coldest part of your refrigerator. You can also place your filled juice jars in the freezer for 10 to 15 minutes to speed the cooling process before transferring them to the refrigerator. (Set a timer so you don't forget about them!)
Add some lemon or lime to your juice blend to help maintain the freshness of your juice.
Common Juicing Problems and Their Solutions
The recipe doesn't produce enough juice: Double the recipe, use more watery vegetables, like cucumbers and celery, or buy a masticating or slow juicer that will produce more juice.
Juice Is Too Thick: Thick juice contains pulp. Strain your juice or clean your juicer to ensure its proper operation.
Juice Is Too Bitter from Greens: Add ½ lemon to the juice to counterbalance the flavor.
Juice Is Too Sweet: Add celery, lemon, or cucumber.

Juicing Precautions

Though juicing provides many benefits, there are a few precautions you should be aware of before starting a juicing regimen:
It is more difficult to measure the calories in liquids than in solid foods—if you aren't careful, you can consume a significant number of calories without realizing it.
Losing weight too quickly on a juicing regimen is unhealthy, and the weight loss you achieve is unlikely to last.
It is always a good idea to wash your produce before you juice it, and you should also consider going completely organic. Commercial produce is often laced with pesticides and fertilizers that can be damaging to your health.
The juice you make at home does not contain any preservatives, so its shelf life is much shorter than store-bought juices. As a result, harmful bacteria may creep into the juice if you don't consume it within a day or two.
If you are fasting while engaging in a juicing regimen, you may experience negative side effects including headaches, dizziness, fatigue, and irritability.

If you are diabetic or have unstable blood sugar, you may want to limit the amount of fruit in your juices and avoid moderate and high glycemic index juices like watermelon, pineapple, and cantaloupe. Monitor your blood glucose and consult with your doctor if you intend to drink fruit-heavy juices. Fortunately, the polyphenols in juice from apples, strawberries, and grapes have been shown to help regulate blood sugar levels.
Pregnant women should avoid juicing large amounts of parsley because it can induce contractions. Additionally, when pregnant or breastfeeding, you should not start a juice fast because it may cause toxins to be released to the baby, either in the womb or through breast milk. However, adding a juice or two to your diet each day will increase your nutrition and hydration. It is recommended that you consult with your doctor before beginning a juicing regimen. Certain individuals, such as those with diabetes, may experience blood-sugar imbalances if they are not careful.

Juicing is an effective way to increase the nutrition in your diet and foster healthier choices. But it's not a magic bullet. Getting yourself some amazing collection of juicing recipes like the ones in this book will be your first step to an exciting way of providing yourself with a full-scale of vitamins, minerals, nutrients, and other microelements and shedding all your excess weight like you never had it. These recipes are tested, nutrient-rich combinations of fruits and vegetables that will help you reach your health goals, you do not have to speculate. So, what are you waiting for? Start juicing already!

Chapter 3
Healthy Morning Juices

Minty Morning Red Juice

Prep time: 5 minutes | Cook time: 0 minutes | Serves 1

1 large beet
1 apple
1 orange
To garnish
sprig of mint
1 thin slice of orange

1. Peel, cut, deseed, and/or chop the ingredients as needed.
2. Place a container under the juicer's spout.
3. Feed the ingredients one at a time, in the order listed, through the juicer.
4. Stir the juice and pour into glasses to serve.

PER SERVING

Calories: 136| Fat: 0g | Protein: 31g | Carbohydrates: 1g | Sugar: 43mg

Pear Limeade Sunrise Juice

Prep time: 5 minutes | Cook time: 0 minutes | Serves 1

½ cup (75 g/3 oz) blueberries
1 cucumber
1 lime
1 pear

1. Peel, cut, deseed, and/or chop the ingredients as needed.
2. Place a container under the juicer's spout.
3. Feed the ingredients one at a time, in the order listed, through the juicer.
4. Stir the juice and pour into glasses to serve.

PER SERVING

Calories: 242| Fat: 0g | Protein: 55g | Carbohydrates: 1g | Sugar: 15mg

Early Apple-Carrot Juice

Prep time: 5 minutes | Cook time: 0 minutes | Serves 2

6 carrots
4 apples
2-inch (5 cm) piece of fresh root ginger

1. Peel, cut, deseed, and/or chop the ingredients as needed.
2. Place a container under the juicer's spout.
3. Feed the ingredients one at a time, in the order listed, through the juicer.
4. Stir the juice and pour into glasses to serve.

PER SERVING

Calories: 262| Fat: 0g | Protein: 1g | Carbohydrates: 33g | Sugar: 20mg

Cinnamon with Potatoes Sunrise Juice

Prep time: 5 minutes | Cook time: 0 minutes | Serves 1

6 large carrots
1½ sweet potatoes
2 red apples
dash of ground cinnamon

1. Peel, cut, deseed, and/or chop the ingredients as needed.
2. Place a container under the juicer's spout.
3. Feed the ingredients one at a time, in the order listed, through the juicer.
4. Stir the juice and pour into glasses to serve.

PER SERVING

Calories: 355| Fat: 0g | Protein: 81g | Carbohydrates: 1g | Sugar: 236mg

Minty Cucumber Limeade with Carrot

Prep time: 10 minutes | Cook time: 0 minutes | Serves 2

8 carrots
2 cucumbers
4 apples
1 lime
Large handful of fresh mint
2-inch (5 cm) piece of fresh root ginger

1. Peel, cut, deseed, and or chop the ingredients as needed.
2. Place a container under the juicer's spout.
3. Feed the ingredients one at a time, in the order listed, through the juicer.
4. Stir the juice and pour into glasses to serve.

PER SERVING

Calories: 267| Fat: 0g | Protein: 60g | Carbohydrates: 1g | Sugar: 120mg

Juicy Cucumber with Parsley

Prep time: 5 minutes | Cook time: 0 minutes | Serves 2

4 apples
4 cucumbers
16 kale leaves
2 handfuls of parsley

1. Peel, cut, deseed, and/or chop the ingredients as needed.
2. Place a container under the juicer's spout.
3. Feed the ingredients one at a time, in the order listed, through the juicer.
4. Stir the juice and pour into glasses to serve.

PER SERVING

Calories: 278| Fat: 0g | Protein: 58g | Carbohydrates: 2g | Sugar: 70mg

Kale with Celery and Cucumber Refresher

Prep time: 5 minutes | Cook time: 0 minutes | Serves 2

10 kale leaves
2 cucumbers
6 celery sticks
2 pears

1. Peel, cut, deseed, and/or chop the ingredients as needed.
2. Place a container under the juicer's spout.
3. Feed the ingredients one at a time, in the order listed, through the juicer.
4. Stir the juice and pour into glasses to serve.

PER SERVING

Calories: 151| Fat: 0g | Protein: 33g | Carbohydrates: 1g | Sugar: 91mg

Pear with Celery Root Refresher

Prep time: 5 minutes | Cook time: 0 minutes | Serves 1

3 celery roots
2 pears

1. Peel, cut, deseed, and/or chop the ingredients as needed.
2. Place a container under the juicer's spout.
3. Feed the ingredients one at a time, in the order listed, through the juicer.
4. Stir the juice and pour into glasses to serve.

PER SERVING

Calories: 328| Fat: 0g | Protein: 78g | Carbohydrates: 2g | Sugar: 440mg

Cabbage with Crispy Pear and Lettuce

Prep time: 5 minutes | Cook time: 0 minutes | Serves 1

1 head of green cabbage
4 small pears
12 romaine lettuce leaves
2-inch (5 cm) piece of fresh root ginger

1. Peel, cut, deseed, and/or chop the ingredients as needed.
2. Place a container under the juicer's spout.
3. Feed the ingredients one at a time, in the order listed, through the juicer.
4. Stir the juice and pour into glasses to serve.

PER SERVING

Calories: 238| Fat: 0g | Protein: 51g | Carbohydrates: 1g | Sugar: 65mg

Chard with Cabbage Refresher

Prep time: 10 minutes | Cook time: 0 minutes | Serves 2

½ head of green cabbage
16 chard leaves
6 carrots
2 apples
2-inch (5 cm) piece of fresh root ginger

1. Peel, cut, deseed, and/or chop the ingredients as needed.
2. Place a container under the juicer's spout.
3. Feed the ingredients one at a time, in the order listed, through the juicer.
4. Stir the juice and pour into glasses to serve.

PER SERVING

Calories: 194| Fat: 0g | Protein: 40g | Carbohydrates: 1g | Sugar: 310mg

Juicy Morning Dew

Prep time: 5 minutes | Cook time: 0 minutes | Serves 1

8 kale leaves
1 small honeydew melon
2 large cucumbers
2 handfuls of parsley

1. Peel, cut, deseed, and/or chop the ingredients as needed.
2. Place a container under the juicer's spout.
3. Feed the ingredients one at a time, in the order listed, through the juicer.
4. Stir the juice and pour into glasses to serve.

PER SERVING

Calories: 209| Fat: 0g | Protein: 44g | Carbohydrates: 1g | Sugar: 103mg

Limey Tomato with Spiced Gazpacho

Prep time: 5 minutes | Cook time: 0 minutes | Serves 1

8 plum tomatoes
2 large cucumbers
4 celery sticks
2 sweet red (bell) peppers
¼ small red onion
3 large handfuls of parsley
2 limes (optional)
sea salt and freshly ground pepper

1. Peel, cut, deseed, and/or chop the ingredients as needed.
2. Place a container under the juicer's spout.
3. Feed the ingredients one at a time, in the order listed, through the juicer.
4. Stir the juice and pour into glasses to serve.

PER SERVING

Calories: 111| Fat: 0g | Protein: 20g | Carbohydrates: 1g | Sugar: 89mg

Lemon and Lime Daily Refresher

Prep time: 10 minutes | Cook time: 0 minutes | Serves 2

2 sweet red (bell) peppers
2 apples
2 tomatoes
2 scallions
3 kale leaves
small handful of sunflower sprouts (optional)
1 lemon
1 lime
Pinch of oregano and ground chili pepper, for sprinkling, or add a dash of fresh oregano and red chili pepper to the juicer

1. Peel, cut, deseed, and/or chop the ingredients as needed.
2. Place a container under the juicer's spout.
3. Feed the ingredients one at a time, in the order listed, through the juicer.
4. Stir the juice and pour into glasses to serve.

PER SERVING

Calories: 146| Fat: 0g | Protein: 32g | Carbohydrates: 1g | Sugar: 20mg

Pear with Ginger Drink

Prep time: 5 minutes | Cook time: 0 minutes | Serves 1

3 parsnips
1 pear
1.5-inch (4 cm) ginger

1. Peel, cut, deseed, and/or chop the ingredients as needed.
2. Place a container under the juicer's spout.
3. Feed the ingredients one at a time, in the order listed, through the juicer.
4. Stir the juice and pour into glasses to serve.

PER SERVING

Calories: 380| Fat: 0g | Protein: 98g | Carbohydrates: 2g | Sugar: 38mg

Juicy Green Cabbage with Lemon

Prep time: 5 minutes | Cook time: 0 minutes | Serves 2

½ head of green cabbage
6 carrots
8 celery sticks
2 apples
1 lemon

1. Peel, cut, deseed, and/or chop the ingredients as needed.
2. Place a container under the juicer's spout.
3. Feed the ingredients one at a time, in the order listed, through the juicer.
4. Stir the juice and pour into glasses to serve.

PER SERVING

Calories: 189| Fat: 0g | Protein: 40g | Carbohydrates: 1g | Sugar: 194mg

Cucumber with Pear and Kale Drink

Prep time: 10 minutes | Cook time: 0 minutes | Serves 1

2 cucumbers
8 carrots
6 kale leaves
1 pear
2-inch (5 cm) piece of fresh root ginger

1. Peel, cut, deseed, and/or chop the ingredients as needed.
2. Place a container under the juicer's spout.
3. Feed the ingredients one at a time, in the order listed, through the juicer.
4. Stir the juice and pour into glasses to serve.

PER SERVING

Calories: 178| Fat: 0g | Protein: 42g | Carbohydrates: 1g | Sugar: 194mg

Juicy Fennel and Celery Drink

Prep time: 5 minutes | Cook time: 0 minutes | Serves 1

10 kale leaves
2 large cucumbers
1 fennel bulb, plus fronds
4 pears
4 celery sticks

1. Peel, cut, deseed, and/or chop the ingredients as needed.
2. Place a container under the juicer's spout.
3. Feed the ingredients one at a time, in the order listed, through the juicer.
4. Stir the juice and pour into glasses to serve.

PER SERVING

Calories: 254| Fat: 0g | Protein: 55g | Carbohydrates: 1g | Sugar: 111mg

Berry with Watermelon Delight

Prep time: 5 minutes | Cook time: 0 minutes | Serves 2

½ watermelon (about 4 cups (400 g/6 oz) chopped)
4 cups (550 g/20 oz) blueberries
16 chard leaves

1. Peel, cut, deseed, and/or chop the ingredients as needed.
2. Place a container under the juicer's spout.
3. Feed the ingredients one at a time, in the order listed, through the juicer.
4. Stir the juice and pour into glasses to serve.

PER SERVING

Calories: 136| Fat: 0g | Protein: 30g | Carbohydrates: 1g | Sugar: 103mg

Lemony Carrot and Apple Morning Drink

Prep time: 5 minutes | Cook time: 0 minutes | Serves 1

4 apples
4 carrots
2 lemons

1. Peel, cut, deseed, and/or chop the ingredients as needed.
2. Place a container under the juicer's spout.
3. Feed the ingredients one at a time, in the order listed, through the juicer.
4. Stir the juice and pour into glasses to serve.

PER SERVING

Calories: 188| Fat: 0g | Protein: 44g | Carbohydrates: 1g | Sugar: 58mg

Berry with Cucumber Beets

Prep time: 5 minutes | Cook time: 0 minutes | Serves 2

1 medium golden or red beet
½ lemon
1 cup raspberries
2 large cucumbers

1. Peel, cut, deseed, and/or chop the ingredients as needed.
2. Place a container under the juicer's spout.
3. Feed the ingredients one at a time, in the order listed, through the juicer.
4. Stir the juice and pour into glasses to serve.

PER SERVING

Calories: 341| Fat: 1g | Protein: 7g | Carbohydrates: 81g | Sugar: 65mg

Juicy Asparagus with Zucchini Drink

Prep time: 5 minutes | Cook time: 0 minutes | Serves 1

½ cucumber
1 zucchini
Handful of parsley
6 asparagus spears (stalks)
1 large tomato
1 apple
30 black/purple or red grapes

1. Peel, cut, deseed, and/or chop the ingredients as needed.
2. Place a container under the juicer's spout.
3. Feed the ingredients one at a time, in the order listed, through the juicer.
4. Stir the juice and pour into glasses to serve.

PER SERVING

Calories: 238| Fat: 0g | Protein: 49g | Carbohydrates: 1g | Sugar: 44mg

Peach and Apple Morning Delight

Prep time: 5 minutes | Cook time: 0 minutes | Serves 1

1 sweet potato
2 ripe peaches (or use pears)
1 apple
1⅓ cups (150 g/6 oz) blueberries
dash of ground cinnamon

1. Peel, cut, deseed, and/or chop the ingredients as needed.
2. Place a co\'ntainer under the juicer's spout.
3. Feed the ingredients one at a time, in the order listed, through the juicer.
4. Stir the juice and pour into glasses to serve.

PER SERVING

Calories: 352| Fat: 0g | Protein: 83g | Carbohydrates: 1g | Sugar: 51mg

Kale with Parsley Morning Drink

Prep time: 5 minutes | Cook time: 0 minutes | Serves 1

3 pears
3 celery sticks
4 kale leaves
Large handful of parsley

1. Peel, cut, deseed, and/or chop the ingredients as needed.
2. Place a container under the juicer's spout.
3. Feed the ingredients one at a time, in the order listed, through the juicer.
4. Stir the juice and pour into glasses to serve.

PER SERVING

Calories: 282| Fat: 0g | Protein: 63g | Carbohydrates: 1g | Sugar: 107mg

Juicy Grapefruit and Orange Drink

Prep time: 5 minutes | Cook time: 0 minutes | Serves 1

2 beets
6 to 8 kale leaves
1 ruby grapefruit
2 oranges

1. Peel, cut, deseed, and/or chop the ingredients as needed.
2. Place a container under the juicer's spout.
3. Feed the ingredients one at a time, in the order listed, through the juicer.
4. Stir the juice and pour into glasses to serve.

PER SERVING

Calories: 277| Fat: 0g | Protein: 59g | Carbohydrates: 1g | Sugar: 121mg

Lemony Berry with Kale Booster
Prep time: 5 minutes | Cook time: 0 minutes | Serves 2

4 kale leaves
½ lemon
1 cup raspberries
1 large cucumber

1. Peel, cut, deseed, and/or chop the ingredients as needed.
2. Place a container under the juicer's spout.
3. Feed the ingredients one at a time, in the order listed, through the juicer.
4. Stir the juice and pour into glasses to serve.

PER SERVING

Calories: 136| Fat: 0g | Protein: 2g | Carbohydrates: 33g | Sugar: 68mg

Fruity Parsnips with Orange Juice
Prep time: 5 minutes | Cook time: 0 minutes | Serves 2

4 large carrots
4 large parsnips
½ pineapple
2 oranges
2-inch (5 cm) piece of ginger

1. Peel, cut, deseed, and/or chop the ingredients as needed.
2. Place a container under the juicer's spout.
3. Feed the ingredients one at a time, in the order listed, through the juicer.
4. Stir the juice and pour into glasses to serve.

PER SERVING

Calories: 235| Fat: 0g | Protein: 54g | Carbohydrates: 1g | Sugar: 75mg

Cucumber Drink with Green Juice
Prep time: 5 minutes | Cook time: 0 minutes | Serves 1

16 kale leaves
2 cucumbers
8 celery sticks
4 apples
1 lemon
2-inch (5 cm) piece of fresh root ginger

1. Peel, cut, deseed, and/or chop the ingredients as needed.
2. Place a container under the juicer's spout.
3. Feed the ingredients one at a time, in the order listed, through the juicer.
4. Stir the juice and pour into glasses to serve.

PER SERVING

Calories: 251| Fat: 0g | Protein: 251g | Carbohydrates: 1g | Sugar: 128mg

Spicy Orange Sunrise Lemonade
Prep time: 5 minutes | Cook time: 0 minutes | Serves 2

2 oranges
2 sweet red (bell) peppers
6 carrots
1 lemon (optional)

1. Peel, cut, deseed, and/or chop the ingredients as needed.
2. Place a container under the juicer's spout.
3. Feed the ingredients one at a time, in the order listed, through the juicer.
4. Stir the juice and pour into glasses to serve.

PER SERVING

Calories: 131| Fat: 0g | Protein: 28g | Carbohydrates: 1g | Sugar: 85mg

Gingered Chard Red Juice
Prep time: 5 minutes | Cook time: 0 minutes | Serves 1

2 beets
4 carrots
4 oranges
8 chard leaves
2-inch (5 cm) piece of fresh root ginger (optional)

1. Peel, cut, deseed, and/or chop the ingredients as needed.
2. Place a container under the juicer's spout.
3. Feed the ingredients one at a time, in the order listed, through the juicer.
4. Stir the juice and pour into glasses to serve.

PER SERVING

Calories: 159| Fat: 0g | Protein: 34g | Carbohydrates: 1g | Sugar: 196mg

Juicy Spinach with Apple Lemonade
Prep time: 5 minutes | Cook time: 0 minutes | Serves 1

2 apples
4 handfuls of spinach
16 kale leaves
1 cucumber
4 celery sticks
2 lemons

1. Peel, cut, deseed, and/or chop the ingredients as needed.
2. Place a container under the juicer's spout.
3. Feed the ingredients one at a time, in the order listed, through the juicer.
4. Stir the juice and pour into glasses to serve.

PER SERVING

Calories: 176| Fat: 0g | Protein: 35g | Carbohydrates: 1g | Sugar: 114mg

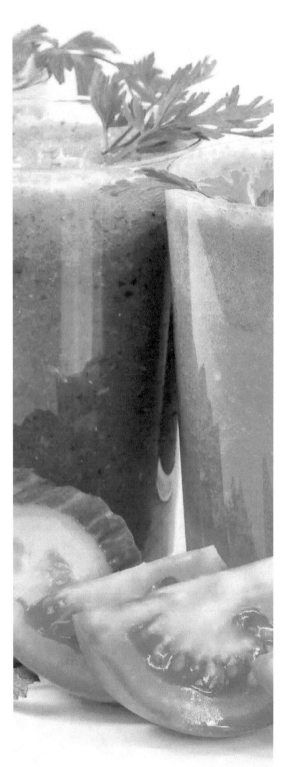

Green Citrus Drink
Prep time: 5 minutes | Cook time: 0 minutes | Serves 1

4 apples
4 oranges
12 handfuls of leafy greens (e.g., kale, chard, spinach, or romaine lettuce)

1. Peel, cut, deseed, and/or chop the ingredients as needed.
2. Place a container under the juicer's spout.
3. Feed the ingredients one at a time, in the order listed, through the juicer.
4. Stir the juice and pour into glasses to serve.

PER SERVING

Calories: 216| Fat: 0g | Protein: 49g | Carbohydrates: 1g | Sugar: 48mg

Juicy Carrot with Ginger and Orange
Prep time: 5 minutes | Cook time: 0 minutes | Serves 1

3 large carrots
2 oranges
2-inch (5 cm) piece of fresh root ginger

1. Peel, cut, deseed, and/or chop the ingredients as needed.
2. Place a container under the juicer's spout.
3. Feed the ingredients one at a time, in the order listed, through the juicer.
4. Stir the juice and pour into glasses to serve.

PER SERVING

Calories: 162| Fat: 0g | Protein: 36g | Carbohydrates: 1g | Sugar: 99mg

Lemony Basil with Celery and Beet
Prep time: 10 minutes | Cook time: 0 minutes | Serves 1

4 beets
2 carrots
6 celery sticks
2 oranges
2 lemon
2 handfuls of basil

1. Peel, cut, deseed, and/or chop the ingredients as needed.
2. Place a container under the juicer's spout.
3. Feed the ingredients one at a time, in the order listed, through the juicer.
4. Stir the juice and pour into glasses to serve.

PER SERVING

Calories: 146| Fat: 0g | Protein: 31g | Carbohydrates: 1g | Sugar: 175mg

Cucumber with Kiwi Berry Blast

Prep time: 10 minutes | Cook time: 0 minutes | Serves 2

1 cup blackberries
1 cup raspberries
2 kiwifruit
1 orange, peeled
2 large celery stalks
1 large cucumber

1. Peel, cut, deseed, and/or chop the ingredients as needed.
2. Place a container under the juicer's spout.
3. Feed the ingredients one at a time, in the order listed, through the juicer.
4. Stir the juice and pour into glasses to serve.

PER SERVING

Calories: 254| Fat: 0g | Protein: 4g | Carbohydrates: 63g | Sugar: 53mg

Juicy Spinach Lemonade

Prep time: 5 minutes | Cook time: 0 minutes | Serves 2

10 kale leaves
2 large handfuls of spinach
6 romaine lettuce leaves
2 cucumbers
6 celery sticks
2 green apples
2 lemons

1. Peel, cut, deseed, and/or chop the ingredients as needed.
2. Place a container under the juicer's spout.
3. Feed the ingredients one at a time, in the order listed, through the juicer.
4. Stir the juice and pour into glasses to serve.

PER SERVING

Calories: 183| Fat: 0g | Protein: 37g | Carbohydrates: 1 | Sugar: 111mg

Berry-Pomegranate with Celery Delight

Prep time: 5 minutes | Cook time: 0 minutes | Serves 2

1 cup blackberries
½ lemon
½ cup pomegranate juice
4 large celery stalks

1. Peel, cut, deseed, and/or chop the ingredients as needed.
2. Place a container under the juicer's spout.
3. Feed the ingredients one at a time, in the order listed, through the juicer.
4. Stir the juice and pour into glasses to serve.

PER SERVING

Calories: 159| Fat: 0g | Protein: 2g | Carbohydrates: 40g | Sugar: 43mg

Kale with Beet Red Juice
Prep time: 5 minutes | Cook time: 0 minutes | Serves 1

2 beets
6 carrots
2 apples
15 kale leaves
2-inch (5 cm) piece of fresh root ginger

1. Peel, cut, deseed, and/or chop the ingredients as needed.
2. Place a container under the juicer's spout.
3. Feed the ingredients one at a time, in the order listed, through the juicer.
4. Stir the juice and pour into glasses to serve.

PER SERVING

Calories: 202| Fat: 0g | Protein: 42g | Carbohydrates: 1g | Sugar: 161mg

Limey Watermelon Crush
Prep time: 5 minutes | Cook time: 0 minutes | Serves 1

½ watermelon (about 4 cups [400 g/6 oz] chopped)
1 lime
handful of basil

1. Peel, cut, deseed, and/or chop the ingredients as needed.
2. Place a container under the juicer's spout.
3. Feed the ingredients one at a time, in the order listed, through the juicer.
4. Stir the juice and pour into glasses to serve.

PER SERVING

Calories: 677| Fat: 0g | Protein: 35g | Carbohydrates: 1g | Sugar: 6mg

Spinach with Basil Refreshing Juice
Prep time: 10 minutes | Cook time: 0 minutes | Serves 2

Handful spinach
2 large Swiss chard leaves
1 cup blueberries
½ lemon
8 large basil leaves
2 large celery stalks

1. Peel, cut, deseed, and/or chop the ingredients as needed.
2. Place a container under the juicer's spout.
3. Feed the ingredients one at a time, in the order listed, through the juicer.
4. Stir the juice and pour into glasses to serve.

PER SERVING

Calories: 118| Fat: 0g | Protein: 1g | Carbohydrates: 30g | Sugar: 38mg

Spicy Lemon with Gingered Juice
Prep time: 5 minutes | Cook time: 0 minutes | Serves 2

1 medium lemon
1-inch piece fresh ginger root (optional)
1 orange bell pepper
4 small oranges, peeled
Alternate ingredients, finishing with the orange.

1. Peel, cut, deseed, and/or chop the ingredients as needed.
2. Place a container under the juicer's spout.
3. Feed the ingredients one at a time, in the order listed, through the juicer.
4. Stir the juice and pour into glasses to serve.

PER SERVING

Calories: 202| Fat: 1g | Protein: 4g | Carbohydrates: 51g | Sugar: 46mg

Spicy Romaine Morning Juice
Prep time: 5 minutes | Cook time: 0 minutes | Serves 2

1 orange, red, or yellow bell pepper
4 romaine leaves
2 small oranges, peeled
1 large cucumber
Alternate ingredients, finishing with the cucumber.

1. Peel, cut, deseed, and/or chop the ingredients as needed.
2. Place a container under the juicer's spout.
3. Feed the ingredients one at a time, in the order listed, through the juicer.
4. Stir the juice and pour into glasses to serve.

PER SERVING

Calories: 106| Fat: 0g | Protein: 3g | Carbohydrates: 24g | Sugar: 16mg

Spinach with Sweet Citrus Juice
Prep time: 10 minutes | Cook time: 0 minutes | Serves 2

Handful spinach
1 large green apple
1 cup pineapple
12 parsley sprigs
1 pink or red grapefruit, peeled

1. Peel, cut, deseed, and/or chop the ingredients as needed.
2. Place a container under the juicer's spout.
3. Feed the ingredients one at a time, in the order listed, through the juicer.
4. Stir the juice and pour into glasses to serve.

PER SERVING

Calories: 176| Fat: 0g | Protein: 2g | Carbohydrates: 45g | Sugar: 49mg

Fennel with Celery Berry Juice

Prep time: 5 minutes | Cook time: 0 minutes | Serves 2

1 large celery stalk
½ fennel bulb
1 cup strawberries
2 medium apples

1. Peel, cut, deseed, and/or chop the ingredients as needed.
2. Place a container under the juicer's spout.
3. Alternate ingredients, finishing with the apple.
4. Stir the juice and pour into glasses to serve.

PER SERVING

Calories: 137| Fat: 0g | Protein: 1g | Carbohydrates: 35g | Sugar: 29mg

Raspberry with Orange Bok Choy

Prep time: 5 minutes | Cook time: 0 minutes | Serves 2

1 large bok choy stem
1 large orange, peeled
1 peach or nectarine, pit removed
1 cup raspberries
1 medium apple

1. Peel, cut, deseed, and/or chop the ingredients as needed.
2. Place a container under the juicer's spout.
3. Alternate ingredients, finishing with the apple.
4. Stir the juice and pour into glasses to serve.

PER SERVING

Calories: 198| Fat: 1g | Protein: 3g | Carbohydrates: 50g | Sugar: 41mg

Morning Cucumber and Berry Chard

Prep time: 5 minutes | Cook time: 0 minutes | Serves 2

1 cup pineapple
1 cup raspberries
2 large celery stalks
2 Swiss chard leaves
½ cucumber

1. Peel, cut, deseed, and/or chop the ingredients as needed.
2. Place a container under the juicer's spout.
3. Feed the ingredients one at a time, in the order listed, through the juicer.
4. Stir the juice and pour into glasses to serve.

PER SERVING

Calories: 200| Fat: 0g | Protein: 2g | Carbohydrates: 51g | Sugar: 45mg

Grapy Kale and Cucumber Delight
Prep time: 10 minutes | Cook time: 0 minutes | Serves 2

1 large celery stalk
2 kale leaves
½ pink or red grapefruit, peeled
1 Cara Cara or other small orange, peeled
½ cup pineapple
½ cucumber

1. Peel, cut, deseed, and/or chop the ingredients as needed.
2. Place a container under the juicer's spout.
3. Feed the ingredients one at a time, in the order listed, through the juicer.
4. Stir the juice and pour into glasses to serve.

PER SERVING

Calories: 65| Fat: 0g | Protein: 1g | Carbohydrates: 16g | Sugar: 14mg

Berry Health Booster
Prep time: 10 minutes | Cook time: 0 minutes | Serves 2

1 kale leaf
4 romaine leaves
Handful spinach
1 green apple
1 cup blueberries
¼ lemon
1 medium cucumber

1. Peel, cut, deseed, and/or chop the ingredients as needed.
2. Place a container under the juicer's spout.
3. Feed the ingredients one at a time, in the order listed, through the juicer.
4. Stir the juice and pour into glasses to serve.

PER SERVING

Calories: 183| Fat: 0g | Protein: 2g | Carbohydrates: 42g | Sugar: 27mg

Lemony Turmeric with Spiced Pineapple
Prep time: 5 minutes | Cook time: 0 minutes | Serves 2
1 yellow bell pepper
½ lemon
1-inch piece fresh ginger root
1-inch piece fresh turmeric root
2 cups pineapple
Freshly ground black pepper (optional)

1. Place a container under the juicer's spout.
2. Feed the ingredients one at a time, in the order listed, through the juicer.
3. Stir the black pepper (if using) directly into the juice to increase your absorption of the curcumin in the turmeric.

PER SERVING

Calories: 177| Fat: 0g | Protein: 2g | Carbohydrates: 46g | Sugar: 36mg

Carroty Breakfast Grind

Prep time: 10 minutes | Cook time: 0 minutes | Serves 3

2 lemons, peeled, seeded, and quartered
2 carrots, chopped
2 apples, peeled and quartered
2 beets, trimmed and chopped
2 cups fresh spinach

1. Press all ingredients through a juicer into a glass or pitcher.

PER SERVING

Calories: 115 | Fat: 0.5g | Protein: 2g | Carbohydrates: 29g
| Sugar: 19mg

Juicy Morning Blaster

Prep time: 10 minutes | Cook time: 0 minutes | Serves 2

1 whole cucumber
2 green apples
3 celery stalks
2 oranges
½ bunch of spinach

1. Wash all produce. Quarter apples and remove all seeds.
2. Peel oranges and remove all seeds.
3. Roll spinach leaves to fit into your juicer.
4. Blend all produce together in your juicer.
5. This can be blended with or served over ice if desired.
6. Stir and drink immediately.

PER SERVING

Calories: 231 | Fat: 1g | Protein: 6g | Carbohydrates: 56g
| Sugar: 21mg

Fresh Morning Juice

Prep time: 10 minutes | Cook time: 0 minutes | Serves 2

1 cup pineapple, cut into chunks
1 green apple, quartered
1 cup fresh spinach
1 leaf kale
1 avocado, peeled and pitted

1. Press all ingredients through a juicer into a large glass.
2. Stir before serving.

PER SERVING

Calories: 286 | Fat: 15g | Protein: 3g | Carbohydrates: 41g
| Sugar: 28mg

Early-Berry Juice

Prep time: 10 minutes | Cook time: 0 minutes | Serves 4

3 large apples
3 large pears
3 blood oranges
2 cups fresh cranberries

1. Prep your pears and apples by cutting them down into small enough chunks for your juicer to easily handle.
2. Peel your oranges and cut them into sixths.
3. Add your apples, oranges, and pears to the juicer, then add the cranberries and stir.
4. Store in a container for up to one week, and serve!

PER SERVING

Calories: 329 | Fat: 1g | Protein: 3g | Carbohydrates: 85g | Sugar: 49mg

Rise & Shine Morning Juice

Prep time: 10 minutes | Cook time: 0 minutes | Serves 2

1 beet, peeled
2 carrots, roughly peeled
1 cup pineapple
1 lemon

1. Cut veggies and fruit into pieces small enough to fit in juicer.
2. Remove visible seeds from lemon but keep peel on it for an extra zip.
3. Slowly add produce to juicer, one by one, until you've juiced it all!
4. Enjoy chilled.

PER SERVING

Calories: 114 | Fat: 0.3g | Protein: 2g | Carbohydrates: 29g | Sugar: 23mg

Homemade Morning Reboot

Prep time: 10 minutes | Cook time: 0 minutes | Serves 2

½ bunch of spinach
3 kale leaves
2 green apples
⅓ of a pineapple
1 orange
½ of a medium cucumber

1. Wash all produce. Roll spinach and kale leaves to fit into your juicer. Quarter green apples and remove all seeds.
2. Dice pineapple into small cubes. Peel orange and remove all seeds. Place all produce into your juicer and blend.
3. This can be blended with or served over ice if desired. Stir and drink immediately.

PER SERVING

Calories: 188 | Fat: 1g | Protein: 5g | Carbohydrates: 46g | Sugar: 23mg

Celery with Broccoli and Sweet Potato
Prep time: 5 minutes | Cook time: 0 minutes | Serves 2

2-inch piece broccoli stem
4 large celery stalks
1 small sweet potato, peeled
½ lemon
1-inch piece fresh turmeric root
3 small oranges, peeled
Freshly ground black pepper (optional)

1. Place a container under the juicer's spout.
2. Feed the ingredients one at a time, in the order listed, through the juicer.
3. Stir the black pepper (if using) directly into the juice to increase your absorption of the curcumin in the turmeric.

PER SERVING

Calories: 35| Fat: 0g | Protein: 1g | Carbohydrates: 8g | Sugar: 3mg

Minty Kiwi with Berry and Apple
Prep time: 5 minutes | Cook time: 0 minutes | Serves 2

½ large cucumber
2 kiwifruit
1 cup raspberries
4 teaspoons fresh mint
1 medium green apple

1. Peel, cut, deseed, and/or chop the ingredients as needed.
2. Place a container under the juicer's spout.
3. Feed the ingredients one at a time, in the order listed, through the juicer.
4. Stir the juice and pour into glasses to serve.

PER SERVING

Calories: 172| Fat: 0g | Protein: 2g | Carbohydrates: 44g | Sugar: 36mg

Orange with Juicy Beet and Carrot
Prep time: 5 minutes | Cook time: 0 minutes | Serves 1

3 beets
8 carrots
3 oranges

1. Peel, cut, deseed, and/or chop the ingredients as needed.
2. Place a container under the juicer's spout.
3. Feed the ingredients one at a time, in the order listed, through the juicer.
4. Stir the juice and pour into glasses to serve.

PER SERVING

Calories: 172| Fat: 0g | Protein: 38g | Carbohydrates: 1g | Sugar: 172mg

Fresh Sunrise Drink

Prep time: 10 minutes | Cook time: 0 minutes | Serves 4

1 Pineapple peeled
4 carrots washed
1 apple red or green
1 lemon juiced separately with a citrus juicer
1 lime

1. Pineapple is known to clog some models of juicers, alternate with carrots and apple. Sitr in fresh squeezed lemon juice.

PER SERVING

Calories: 174 | Fat: 1g | Protein: 2g | Carbohydrates: 45g | Sugar: 30mg

Juicy Morning Glow

Prep time: 10 minutes | Cook time: 0 minutes | Serves 3

2 small, sweet potatoes
3 carrots
3 (organic) apples
4 mandarin oranges
A small piece of fresh ginger

1. Peel the sweet potatoes and carrots and cut them into small cubes.
2. Rinse the apples and peel the mandarins and ginger.
3. Cut the fruit into smaller pieces as well. Juice all the ingredients, pour into to glasses, and enjoy!
4. The juice can be stored in the fridge for 2 to 3 days.

PER SERVING

Calories: 290 | Fat: 1g | Protein: 5g | Carbohydrates: 72g | Sugar: 24mg

Limey Morning Blast

Prep time: 10 minutes | Cook time: 0 minutes | Serves 2

1 organic English cucumber with skin on
1 handful spinach
1 bunch organic celery
1 lime, peeled
1 lemon, peeled
1-inch fresh ginger, peeled

1. Using a slow juicer or a juice of your choice, run each piece of fruit and vegetable through the juicer one at a time until everything has been juiced.
2. Enjoy!
3. Juice is best enjoyed immediately or store in an airtight glass container for up to 1 day.

PER SERVING

Calories: 40 | Fat: 0.3g | Protein: 1.4g | Carbohydrates: 10g | Sugar: 4mg

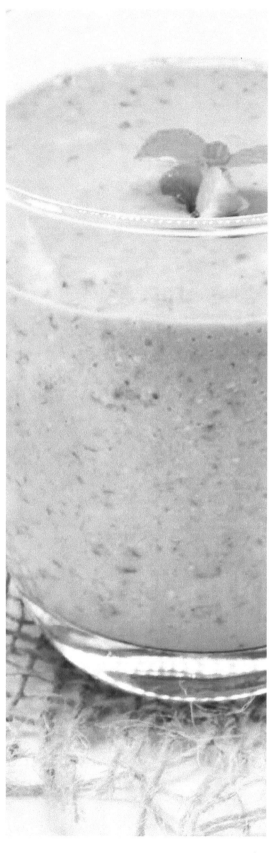

Chapter 4
Fruit-Based Juices

Carrot with Grapefruit Juice
Prep time: 5 minutes | Cook time: 0 minutes | Serves 1

2 grapefruits, peeled
1 red bell pepper
2 pears
6 carrots

1. Thoroughly wash the carrots, pears and grapefruits, peel and cut into chunks. Throw into a juicer along with red pepper.
2. Process and drink immediately.

PER SERVING

Calories: 90| Fat: 2g | Protein: 1g | Carbohydrates: 19g | Sugar: 5mg

Berries with Apple Juice
Prep time: 5 minutes | Cook time: 0 minutes | Serves 2

3 apples, cored
1 cup of cranberry juice
1 cup of fresh blueberries

1. Process the apples and blueberries through a juicer and pour into a pitcher.
2. Add the cranberry juice, stir well, and enjoy over ice.

PER SERVING

Calories: 120| Fat: 0g | Protein: 0g | Carbohydrates: 30g | Sugar: 15mg

Limey Pineapple Chili
Prep time: 5 minutes | Cook time: 0 minutes | Serves 1

½ pineapple
½ lime, peeled
7 long carrots
½ small chili

1. Remove the rind from the lime.
2. Trim the ends of carrots and discard the greens. Run through a juicer along with lime, pineapple, and chili.
3. Pour into a tall glass, add 2 to 3 cubes of ice and drink immediately.

PER SERVING

Calories: 262| Fat: 0g | Protein: 1g | Carbohydrates: 33g | Sugar: 20mg

Berry Basil Juice
Prep time: 5 minutes | Cook time: 0 minutes | Serves 2

3 ripe tomatoes, cut into quarters
2 cups of strawberries
2 to 3 basil leaves

1. Wash the strawberries, tomatoes and basil leaves and process through a juicer.
2. Pour into a glass over ice, garnish with a basil leave and serve.

PER SERVING

Calories: 241| Fat: 6.8g | Protein: 9.3g | Carbohydrates: 42g | Sugar: 275mg

Gingered Apple Lemonade
Prep time: 5 minutes | Cook time: 0 minutes | Serves 2

½ lemon
3 apples, quartered
1 yellow pepper, cut into chunks
1-inch piece of ginger root

1. Core the apples and cut into quarters. Remove the seeds from the pepper.
2. Add all the ingredients to a juicer and process.
3. Drink immediately.

PER SERVING

Calories: 170| Fat: 0g | Protein: 0g | Carbohydrates: 41g | Sugar: 35mg

Berry with Ginger Juice
Prep time: 5 minutes | Cook time: 0 minutes | Serves 1

2 to 3 apples, quartered
8 oz. (230 g) blackberries
½-inch fresh ginger

1. Peel the apples, cut into quarters, and pass through a juicer along with ginger and blackberries.
2. Pour the juice into a glass, stir well and drink immediately.

PER SERVING

Calories: 170| Fat: 0g | Protein: 0g | Carbohydrates: 41g | Sugar: 35mg

Apricot with Avocado and Carrot Juice

Prep time: 5 minutes | Cook time: 0 minutes | Serves 1

½ avocado
1 large carrot
1 orange
1 fresh or dried apricot

1. Peel the carrot and orange and run through a juicer.
2. Pour the extracted juice into a blender, add the avocado and fresh or dried apricot and pulse until smooth.
3. Enjoy over ice.

PER SERVING

Calories: 280| Fat: 3g | Protein: 55g | Carbohydrates: 39g | Sugar: 90mg

Cinnamon with Hot Apple Juice

Prep time: 5 minutes | Cook time: 0 minutes | Serves 1

3 apples
A pinch of cinnamon

1. Wash the apples, core, and cut into quarters.
2. Add to a juicer and juice. Pour the juice into a small pot and heat over low heat. Make sure not to boil.
3. Pour the hot juice into a cup, sprinkle with cinnamon and enjoy.

PER SERVING

Calories: 286| Fat: 1g | Protein: 1g | Carbohydrates: 76g | Sugar: 6mg

Minty Cucumber with Watermelon

Prep time: 5 minutes | Cook time: 0 minutes | Serves 1

4 cups watermelon, cubed
½ lime
¼ orange
½ cucumber, unpeeled
4 to 5 sprigs of mint (or to taste)

1. Peel the orange and lime and run through a juicer along with mint and cucumber.
2. Finally, juice the watermelon.
3. Pour the juice into a tall glass over ice, stir well, decorate with mint, and serve.

PER SERVING

Calories: 224| Fat: 1g | Protein: 5g | Carbohydrates: 56g | Sugar: 10mg

Celery with Fennel and Mango Juice

Prep time: 5 minutes | Cook time: 0 minutes | Serves 1

1 mango
1 apple
2 leaves romaine lettuce
1 peach
1 fennel
1 celery stalk
½ thumb size piece of ginger

1. Run the mango, fennel, apple, peach, celery, and ginger through a juicer.
2. Pour into a glass, stir well and drink immediately.

PER SERVING

Calories: 470| Fat: 2g | Protein: 9g | Carbohydrates: 116g | Sugar: 148mg

Lemony Sweet and Sour Juice

Prep time: 5 minutes | Cook time: 0 minutes | Serves 1

1 mango
½ lemon, peeled
1 cup of blueberries
3 to 4 middle-sized strawberries

1. Peel the lemon and put in a juicer followed by the blueberries, mango, and strawberries.
2. Pour the juice into a glass and enjoy.

PER SERVING

Calories: 414| Fat: 2g | Protein: 4g | Carbohydrates: 105g | Sugar: 6mg

Apple with Cherry and Pear Juice

Prep time: 5 minutes | Cook time: 0 minutes | Serves 1

1 apple
1 pear
½ cup of cherries

1. Wash the pear, apple, and cherries, remove the pits and run through a juicer.
2. Enjoy over ice.

PER SERVING

Calories: 139| Fat: 0g | Protein: 1g | Carbohydrates: 36g | Sugar: 10mg

Mixed Berry with Cucumber Super Juice
Prep time: 5 minutes | Cook time: 0 minutes | Serves 1

1 cup raspberries
1 cup strawberries
½ cup blackberries
1 cucumber
½ cup blueberries

1. Wash the berries and cucumber and pass through a juicer.
2. Drink immediately.

PER SERVING

Calories: 207| Fat: 2g | Protein: 5g | Carbohydrates: 47g | Sugar: 8mg

Grapy Berry with Apple Juice
Prep time: 5 minutes | Cook time: 0 minutes | Serves 2

1 ripe grapefruit
1 cup blueberries
1 cup red grapes
1 small apple

1. Peel, cut, deseed, and/or chop the ingredients as needed.
2. Place a container under the juicer's spout.
3. Feed the ingredients one at a time, in the order listed, through the juicer.
4. Stir the juice and pour into glasses to serve.

PER SERVING

Calories: 489| Fat: 2g | Protein: 5g | Carbohydrates: 125g | Sugar: 12mg

Quick and Simple Celery Juice
Prep time: 5 minutes | Cook time: 0 minutes | Serves 2

3 medium apples
2 medium stalks celery
2 tablespoons freshly squeezed lime juice

1. Peel, cut, deseed, and/or chop the ingredients as needed.
2. Place a container under the juicer's spout.
3. Feed the apples and celery through the juicer.
4. Stir the lime juice into the juice and pour into glasses to serve.

PER SERVING

Calories: 297| Fat: 1g | Protein: 2g | Carbohydrates: 79g | Sugar: 33mg

Beet with Berry and Apple Juice
Prep time: 5 minutes | Cook time: 0 minutes | Serves 2

2 cups blueberries
2 small beets
1 small apple

1. Peel, cut, deseed, and/or chop the ingredients as needed.
2. Place a container under the juicer's spout.
3. Feed the ingredients one at a time, in the order listed, through the juicer.
4. Stir the juice and pour into glasses to serve.

PER SERVING

Calories: 317| Fat: 2g | Protein: 5g | Carbohydrates: 79g | Sugar: 132mg

Limey Cilantro Gazpacho Juice
Prep time: 5 minutes | Cook time: 0 minutes | Serves 2

2 ripe plum tomatoes
1 ripe mango
½ small orange bell pepper
½ lime
3 sprigs cilantro

1. Peel, cut, deseed, and/or chop the ingredients as needed.
2. Place a container under the juicer's spout.
3. Feed the ingredients one at a time, in the order listed, through the juicer.
4. Stir the juice and pour into glasses to serve.

PER SERVING

Calories: 240| Fat: 2g | Protein: 5g | Carbohydrates: 59g | Sugar: 15mg

Parsley with Limey Orange Juice
Prep time: 5 minutes | Cook time: 0 minutes | Serves 2

1 medium navel orange
1 medium apple
1 medium pear
½ bunch parsley
½ lime

1. Peel, cut, deseed, and/or chop the ingredients as needed.
2. Place a container under the juicer's spout.
3. Feed the ingredients one at a time, in the order listed, through the juicer.
4. Stir the juice and pour into glasses to serve.

PER SERVING

Calories: 100| Fat: 0g | Protein: 1g | Carbohydrates: 27g | Sugar: 2mg

Kiwi and Sparkling Pineapple Juice
Prep time: 5 minutes | Cook time: 0 minutes | Serves 2

1 small pineapple
3 ripe kiwis
1 cup sparkling water

1. Peel, cut, deseed, and/or chop the ingredients as needed.
2. Place a container under the juicer's spout.
3. Feed the pineapple and kiwis through the juicer.
4. Stir the sparkling water into the juice and pour into glasses to serve.

PER SERVING

Calories: 233| Fat: 1g | Protein: 3g | Carbohydrates: 60g | Sugar: 56mg

Lemony Mango with Cantaloupe Juice
Prep time: 5 minutes | Cook time: 0 minutes | Serves 2

2 ripe mangoes
2 cups watermelon
1 cup cantaloupe
1 tablespoon freshly squeezed lemon juice

1. Peel, cut, deseed, and/or chop the ingredients as needed.
2. Place a container under the juicer's spout.
3. Feed the mangoes, watermelon, and cantaloupe through the juicer.
4. Stir the lemon juice into the juice and pour into glasses to serve.

PER SERVING

Calories: 280| Fat: 1g | Protein: 4g | Carbohydrates: 70g | Sugar: 19mg

Cold Strawberry Lemonade
Prep time: 5 minutes | Cook time: 0 minutes | Serves 4

1 cup strawberries
3 lemons
3 cups cold water
1 tablespoon raw honey (optional)

1. Peel, cut, deseed, and/or chop the ingredients as needed.
2. Place a container under the juicer's spout.
3. Feed the strawberries and lemons through the juicer.
4. Stir the water and honey into the juice and pour into glasses to serve.

PER SERVING

Calories: 35| Fat: 0g | Protein: 0g | Carbohydrates: 10g | Sugar: 4mg

Minty Berry Mix Blast
Prep time: 5 minutes | Cook time: 0 minutes | Serves 2

2 cups blueberries
1 cup strawberries
1 cup raspberries
½ cup currants (optional)
1 bunch mint leaves

1. Peel, cut, deseed, and/or chop the ingredients as needed.
2. Place a container under the juicer's spout.
3. Feed the ingredients one at a time, in the order listed, through the juicer.
4. Stir the juice and pour into glasses to serve.

PER SERVING

Calories: 380| Fat: 1g | Protein: 3g | Carbohydrates: 96g | Sugar: 13mg

Berry with Cilantro and Banana Juice
Prep time: 5 minutes | Cook time: 0 minutes | Serves 2

2 cups strawberries
1 cup cilantro
1 cup cold water
1 small banana

1. Peel, cut, deseed, and/or chop the ingredients as needed.
2. Place a container under the juicer's spout.
3. Feed the strawberries and cilantro through the juicer.
4. In a blender, combine the water and banana and blend until smooth.
5. Add the strawberry cilantro juice and pulse to blend.
6. Pour into glasses and serve.

PER SERVING

Calories: 92| Fat: 1g | Protein: 2g | Carbohydrates: 23g | Sugar: 8mg

Cilantro Kiwi Juice Blend
Prep time: 5 minutes | Cook time: 0 minutes | Serves 2

2 cups blackberries
2 ripe kiwis
1 medium apple
6 sprigs cilantro

1. Peel, cut, deseed, and/or chop the ingredients as needed.
2. Place a container under the juicer's spout.
3. Feed the ingredients one at a time, in the order listed, through the juicer.
4. Stir the juice and pour into glasses to serve.

PER SERVING

Calories: 284| Fat: 1g | Protein: 3g | Carbohydrates: 72g | Sugar: 12mg

Berry with Sparkling Pomegranate Juice
Prep time: 5 minutes | Cook time: 0 minutes | Serves 2

2 cups raspberries
2 ripe pomegranates
1 cup sparkling water

1. Peel and remove the seeds from the pomegranate.
2. Place a container under the juicer's spout.
3. Feed the raspberries and pomegranate seeds through the juicer.
4. Stir the sparkling water into the juice and pour into glasses to serve.

PER SERVING

Calories: 467| Fat: 4g | Protein: 6g | Carbohydrates: 113g | Sugar: 19mg

Lavender with Pineapple Juice
Prep time: 5 minutes | Cook time: 0 minutes | Serves 2

1 pineapple
1 tablespoon lavender blossoms

1. Peel, cut, deseed, and/or chop the ingredients as needed.
2. Place a container under the juicer's spout.
3. Feed the pineapple through the juicer.
4. Using a mortar and pestle, grind the lavender blossoms into a powder.
5. Stir the lavender powder into the pineapple juice and pour into a glass to serve.

PER SERVING

Calories: 226| Fat: 1g | Protein: 2g | Carbohydrates: 59g | Sugar: 5mg

Kale with Honeydew Apple Juice
Prep time: 5 minutes | Cook time: 0 minutes | Serves 2

2 medium apples
1 small honeydew
4 small kale leaves

1. Peel, cut, deseed, and/or chop the ingredients as needed.
2. Place a container under the juicer's spout.
3. Feed the ingredients one at a time, in the order listed, through the juicer.
4. Stir the juice and pour into glasses to serve.

PER SERVING

Calories: 113| Fat: 1g | Protein: 2g | Carbohydrates: 29g | Sugar: 15mg

Berry with Watermelon Juice Blend
Prep time: 5 minutes | Cook time: 0 minutes | Serves 2

3 cups watermelon
2 cups raspberries
1 cup strawberries

1. Peel, cut, deseed, and/or chop the ingredients as needed.
2. Place a container under the juicer's spout.
3. Feed the ingredients one at a time, in the order listed, through the juicer.
4. Stir the juice and pour into glasses to serve.

PER SERVING

Calories: 325| Fat: 1g | Protein: 4g | Carbohydrates: 83g | Sugar: 11mg

Papaya Pineapple Juice Blend
Prep time: 5 minutes | Cook time: 0 minutes | Serves 2

1 small pineapple
1 papaya
1 small apple

1. Peel, cut, deseed, and/or chop the ingredients as needed.
2. Place a container under the juicer's spout.
3. Feed the ingredients one at a time, in the order listed, through the juicer.
4. Stir the juice and pour into glasses to serve.

PER SERVING

Calories: 299| Fat: 1g | Protein: 3g | Carbohydrates: 78g | Sugar: 12mg

Blueberry with Pineapple Juice
Prep time: 5 minutes | Cook time: 0 minutes | Serves 2

1 ½ cups blueberries
1 cup pineapple
1 medium apple

1. Peel, cut, deseed, and/or chop the ingredients as needed.
2. Place a container under the juicer's spout.
3. Feed the ingredients one at a time, in the order listed, through the juicer.
4. Stir the juice and pour into glasses to serve.

PER SERVING

Calories: 470| Fat: 2g | Protein: 9g | Carbohydrates: 116g | Sugar: 12mg

Limey Kiwi with Orange Juice
Prep time: 5 minutes | Cook time: 0 minutes | Serves 2

3 medium navel oranges
3 ripe kiwis
1 teaspoon lime zest

1. Peel, cut, deseed, and/or chop the ingredients as needed.
2. Place a container under the juicer's spout.
3. Feed the oranges and kiwis through the juicer.
4. Stir the lime zest into the juice and pour into glasses to serve.

PER SERVING

Calories: 104| Fat: 0g | Protein: 2g | Carbohydrates: 27g | Sugar: 2mg

Purple Peach & Berry Juice
Prep time: 5 minutes | Cook time: 0 minutes | Serves 2

2 medium peaches
1 medium apple
1 cup blueberries
1 cup parsley leaves

1. Peel, cut, deseed, and/or chop the ingredients as needed.
2. Place a container under the juicer's spout.
3. Feed the ingredients one at a time, in the order listed, through the juicer.
4. Stir the juice and pour into glasses to serve.

PER SERVING

Calories: 229 | Fat: 1g | Protein: 3g | Carbohydrates: 57g | Sugar: 48mg

Limey Jicama Fruit Juice
Prep time: 5 minutes | Cook time: 0 minutes | Serves 2

2 cups jicama
2 medium carrots
1 medium pear
½ lemon
½ lime

1. Peel, cut, deseed, and/or chop the ingredients as needed.
2. Place a container under the juicer's spout.
3. Feed the ingredients one at a time, in the order listed, through the juicer.
4. Stir the juice and pour into glasses to serve.

PER SERVING

Calories: 131 | Fat: 0.4g | Protein: 2g | Carbohydrates: 33g | Sugar: 14mg

Berry Renewal Fruit Juice
Prep time: 5 minutes | Cook time: 0 minutes | Serves 2

2 cups raspberries
1 large carrot
1 medium pear
1 tablespoon freshly squeezed lemon juice

1. Peel, cut, deseed, and/or chop the ingredients as needed.
2. Place a container under the juicer's spout.
3. Feed the raspberries, carrot, and pear through the juicer.
4. Stir the lemon juice into the juice and pour into glasses to serve.

PER SERVING

Calories: 300 | Fat: 0.5g | Protein: 3g | Carbohydrates: 77g | Sugar: 62mg

Rosy Berry Fruit Juice
Prep time: 8 minutes | Cook time: 0 minutes | Serves 4
1 pound strawberries, hulled, plus whole strawberries for serving
$\frac{1}{4}$ cup mint leaves, plus sprigs for serving
2 tablespoon fresh lime juice
2 tablespoon light agave nectar
1 teaspoon rose water (optional)
Club soda and lime wheels (for serving)

1. Purée hulled strawberries, mint leaves, lime juice, agave nectar, rose water (if using), and 2 cups cold water in a blender until smooth.
2. Transfer purée to an airtight container, cover, and chill until cold, about 1 hour.
3. Skim off any foam from surface and pour purée into four 12-oz. glasses filled with ice (glasses should be about two-thirds full).
4. Top off with club soda and garnish with mint sprigs, lime wheels, and whole strawberries.

PER SERVING

Calories: 46 | Fat: 0.4g | Protein: 1g | Carbohydrates: 11g | Sugar: 6mg

Pink Grapey Delight
Prep time: 6 minutes | Cook time: 0 minutes | Serves 2
2 small pink grapefruits
2 limes
1 cup cold water
1 tablespoon raw honey (optional)
1 teaspoon lemon zest

1. Peel, cut, deseed, and/or chop the ingredients as needed.
2. Place a container under the juicer's spout.
3. Feed the grapefruits and limes through the juicer.
4. Stir the water, honey, and lemon zest into the juice and pour into glasses to serve.

PER SERVING

Calories: 107 | Fat: 0.2g | Protein: 1.5g | Carbohydrates: 29g | Sugar: 23mg

Homemade Citrus Blend

Prep time: 5 minutes | Cook time: 0 minutes | Serves 2

2 medium tangerines
1 medium navel orange
½ small pink grapefruit
½ lime
1 cup cold water

1. Peel, cut, deseed, and/or chop the ingredients as needed.
2. Place a container under the juicer's spout.
3. Feed the citrus fruits through the juicer.
4. Stir the water into the juice and pour into glasses to serve.

PER SERVING

Calories: 100 | Fat: 0.4g | Protein: 2g | Carbohydrates: 25g | Sugar: 19mg

Apple Orchard Blend

Prep time: 5 minutes | Cook time: 0 minutes | Serves 2

2 medium golden delicious apples
1 medium granny smith apple
1 medium gala apple
1 medium red delicious apple

1. Peel, cut, deseed, and/or chop the ingredients as needed.
2. Place a container under the juicer's spout.
3. Feed the apples through the juicer.
4. Stir the juice and pour into glasses to serve.

PER SERVING

Calories: 255 | Fat: 1g | Protein: 1.4g | Carbohydrates: 62g | Sugar: 46mg

Carroty Blood Orange Bounty

Prep time: 5 minutes | Cook time: 0 minutes | Serves 2

3 large blood oranges
2 medium apples
1 large carrot
1 large stalk celery

1. Peel, cut, deseed, and/or chop the ingredients as needed.
2. Place a container under the juicer's spout.
3. Feed the ingredients one at a time, in the order listed, through the juicer.
4. Stir the juice and pour into glasses to serve.

PER SERVING

Calories: 240 | Fat: 1g | Protein: 3g | Carbohydrates: 61g | Sugar: 47mg

Minty-Melon Fruit Juice

Prep time: 10 minutes | Cook time: 5 minutes | Serves 6

¼ cup (packed) fresh mint leaves
¼ cup sugar or agave syrup
5 cups peeled, seeded, coarsely chopped watermelon (from about a 2 ½ pound watermelon)
¼ cup fresh lime juice
Mint sprigs (for serving)

1. Combine mint leaves, sugar, and ¼ cup water in a small pot. Bring to a boil and stir until sugar has dissolved.
2. Transfer mixture to a heatproof container and chill, uncovered, until cool, about 30 minutes.
3. Strain mint syrup into a blender; discard mint leaves. Add watermelon and lime juice and blend until very smooth. Using a fine-mesh sieve, strain into a pitcher; discard solids.
4. Add 2 cups water and stir well to combine. Serve with mint sprigs.
5. Aqua fresca can be stored in an airtight container and chilled for up to 1 day.

PER SERVING

Calories: 212 | Fat: 0.4g | Protein: 1g | Carbohydrates: 57g | Sugar: 52mg

Minty Cucumber and Pear Delicious Juice

Prep time: 5 minutes | Cook time: 0 minutes | Serves 2

2 medium pears
1 small cucumber
1 sprig mint

1. Peel, cut, deseed, and/or chop the ingredients as needed.
2. Place a container under the juicer's spout.
3. Feed the ingredients one at a time, in the order listed, through the juicer.
4. Stir the juice and pour into glasses to serve.

PER SERVING

Calories: 202 | Fat: 3g | Protein: 1.5g | Carbohydrates: 46g | Sugar: 32mg

Banana Blackberry Fruit Juice

Prep time: 5 minutes | Cook time: 0 minutes | Serves 2

2 cups blackberries
1 medium apple
1 small banana

1. Peel, cut, deseed, and/or chop the ingredients as needed.
2. Place a container under the juicer's spout.
3. Feed the blackberries and apple through the juicer.
4. In a blender, blend the banana until smooth.
5. Stir the pureed banana into the juice and pour into glasses to serve.

PER SERVING

Calories: 328 | Fat: 1g | Protein: 4g | Carbohydrates: 83g | Sugar: 66mg

Sugared Avocado with Lemon Water

Prep time: 5 minutes | Cook time: 0 minutes | Serves 2

1 avocado, halved
4 cups (950 ml/32 fl oz) water
½ cup (120 ml/4 fl oz) lemon juice or lime juice
½ cup (100 g) sugar, plus more to taste

1.   Scoop the avocado into a blender. Add the rest of the ingredients and blend until smooth.
2.   Add more sugar to taste, if desired. Serve over ice.

PER SERVING

Calories: 271 | Fat: 15g | Protein: 2g | Carbohydrates: 38g | Sugar: 27mg

Juicy Tropical Island

Prep time: 10 minutes | Cook time: 0 minutes | Serves 1

1 large apple
1 large orange (peeled)
1 pinch cayenne pepper (spice)
1 mango (peeled)
½ lemon (peeled)

1.   Wash the fruits and vegetables thoroughly
2.   Put them through juicer and enjoy

PER SERVING

Calories: 245 | Fat: 1g | Protein: 4g | Carbohydrates: 73g | Sugar: 41mg

Homemade Avocado Juice

Prep time: 5 minutes | Cook time: 0 minutes | Serves 1

1 medium avocado, pitted and peeled
3 medium peaches, pitted and peeled
¼ cup Greek yogurt

1.   Slice up the peaches and avocado and throw them in the blender.
2.   Add the yogurt to the blender.
3.   Process together the three ingredients in a blender.
4.   This incredible combination is not only delicious but provides many essential nutrients. The avocado is jam-packed with essential oils and fats. Despite popular belief, these healthy fats are an important key in fat loss.

PER SERVING

Calories: 522 | Fat: 30g | Protein: 12g | Carbohydrates: 62g | Sugar: 40g

Heavenly Fruit Juice

Prep time: 10 minutes | Cook time: 0 minutes | Serves 2

5-6 blueberries
4 strawberries
2 apples
3-4 pitted dates
Pinch of dulse powder

1.   Remove stems from the apples.
2.   Place all ingredients in a blender.
3.   Blend well and serve fresh.

PER SERVING

Calories: 140 | Fat: 0.4g | Protein: 1g | Carbohydrates: 37g | Sugar: 28mg

Chapter 5
Vegetable-Based Juices

Chili Tomato with Cucumber Juice
Prep time: 5 minutes | Cook time: 0 minutes | Serves 2

6 plum tomatoes
1 medium red bell pepper
1 large carrot
1 small cucumber
1 red chili pepper

1. Peel, cut, deseed, and/or chop the ingredients as needed.
2. Place a container under the juicer's spout.
3. Feed the ingredients one at a time, in the order listed, through the juicer.
4. Stir the juice and pour into glasses to serve.

PER SERVING

Calories: 175| Fat: 1g | Protein: 2g | Carbohydrates: 43g | Sugar: 37mg

Juicy Ginger Beets with Apple
Prep time: 5 minutes | Cook time: 0 minutes | Serves 2

2 medium beets
2 large carrots
1 medium apple
1 cup cold water
1-inch piece gingerroot

1. In a blender, combine all the ingredients and blend until as smooth as possible.
2. Press the mixture through a fine mesh strainer until all the juice is out.
3. Discard the pulp, pour into glasses, and serve.

PER SERVING

Calories: 77| Fat: 0g | Protein: 1g | Carbohydrates: 19g | Sugar: 13mg

Broccoli with Cucumber-Celery Juice
Prep time: 5 minutes | Cook time: 0 minutes | Serves 2

2 large stalks celery
1 small head broccoli
1 cucumber
1 small pear
½ bunch parsley leaves

1. Peel, cut, deseed, and/or chop the ingredients as needed.
2. Place a container under the juicer's spout.
3. Feed the ingredients one at a time, in the order listed, through the juicer.
4. Stir the juice and pour into glasses to serve.

PER SERVING

Calories: 42| Fat: 0g | Protein: 1g | Carbohydrates: 9g | Sugar: 6mg

Juicy Avocado with Spirulina Juice
Prep time: 10 minutes | Cook time: 0 minutes | Serves 2

2 small apples
1 seedless cucumber
1 ripe avocado
1 teaspoon spirulina powder

1. Peel, cut, deseed, and/or chop the ingredients as needed.
2. Place a container under the juicer's spout.
3. Feed the apples and cucumber through the juicer.
4. In a blender or food processor, blend the avocado until smooth.
5. Stir the pureed avocado and spirulina into the juice and pour into glasses to serve.

PER SERVING

Calories: 254| Fat: 15g | Protein: 2g | Carbohydrates: 32g | Sugar: 18mg

Gingered Radish with Juicy Spinach
Prep time: 5 minutes | Cook time: 0 minutes | Serves 2

8 small radishes with greens
2 cups baby spinach leaves
1 large carrot
1 large stalk celery
1 medium apple
½-inch piece gingerroot

1. Peel, cut, deseed, and/or chop the ingredients as needed.
2. Place a container under the juicer's spout.
3. Feed the ingredients one at a time, in the order listed, through the juicer.
4. Stir the juice and pour into glasses to serve.

PER SERVING

Calories: 70| Fat: 0g | Protein: 1g | Carbohydrates: 17g | Sugar: 11mg

Juicy Carrot Refresher
Prep time: 5 minutes | Cook time: 0 minutes | Serves 2

5 medium carrots
3 medium green apples
1 large red bell pepper

1. Peel, cut, deseed, and/or chop the ingredients as needed.
2. Place a container under the juicer's spout.
3. Feed the ingredients one at a time, in the order listed, through the juicer.
4. Stir the juice and pour into glasses to serve.

PER SERVING

Calories: 213| Fat: 0g | Protein: 3g | Carbohydrates: 54g | Sugar: 37mg

Parsley with Tomato Vegetable Juice

Prep time: 5 minutes | Cook time: 0 minutes | Serves 4

6 red radishes with greens
3 plum tomatoes
2 medium beets
2 small carrots
2 large stalks celery
2 cups packed parsley leaves

1. Peel, cut, deseed, and/or chop the ingredients as needed.
2. Place a container under the juicer's spout.
3. Feed the ingredients one at a time, in the order listed, through the juicer.
4. Stir the juice and pour into glasses to serve.

PER SERVING

Calories: 106| Fat: 1g | Protein: 3g | Carbohydrates: 25g | Sugar: 19mg

Juicy Chard with Lemony Cabbage

Prep time: 5 minutes | Cook time: 0 minutes | Serves 4

4 large Swiss chard leaves
2 large carrots
1 medium apple
¼ small head red cabbage
2 tablespoons freshly squeezed lemon juice

1. Peel, cut, deseed, and/or chop the ingredients as needed.
2. Place a container under the juicer's spout.
3. Feed the Swiss chard, carrots, apple, and cabbage through the juicer.
4. Stir the lemon juice into the juice and pour into glasses to serve.

PER SERVING

Calories: 102| Fat: 25g | Protein: 0g | Carbohydrates: 2g | Sugar: 16mg

Kale with Gingerroot and Celery Blend

Prep time: 5 minutes | Cook time: 0 minutes | Serves 2

1 cup baby spinach leaves
1 large carrot
1 large stalk celery
½ bunch kale leaves
½ small cucumber
1 medium apple
1-inch piece gingerroot

1. Peel, cut, deseed, and/or chop the ingredients as needed.
2. Place a container under the juicer's spout.
3. Feed the ingredients one at a time, in the order listed, through the juicer.
4. Stir the juice and pour into glasses to serve.

PER SERVING

Calories: 72| Fat: 0g | Protein: 1g | Carbohydrates: 17g | Sugar: 12mg

Hot Parsley with Onion Juice

Prep time: 10 minutes | Cook time: 0 minutes | Serves 2

4 plum tomatoes
2 large stalks celery
1 seedless cucumber
1 medium carrot
1 small red bell pepper
½ bunch parsley leaves
1 lime
1 green onion

1. Peel, cut, deseed, and/or chop the ingredients as needed.
2. Place a container under the juicer's spout.
3. Feed the ingredients one at a time, in the order listed, through the juicer.
4. Stir the juice and pour into glasses to serve.

PER SERVING

Calories: 136| Fat: 0g | Protein: 2g | Carbohydrates: 31g | Sugar: 26mg

Juicy Spinach Limeade

Prep time: 10 minutes | Cook time: 0 minutes | Serves 2

2 bunches spinach leaves
1 medium green apple
1 lime

1. Peel, cut, deseed, and/or chop the ingredients as needed.
2. Place a container under the juicer's spout.
3. Feed the ingredients one at a time, in the order listed, through the juicer.
4. Stir the juice and pour into glasses to serve.

PER SERVING

Calories: 121| Fat: 2g | Protein: 10g | Carbohydrates: 26g | Sugar: 11mg

Fennel with Celery Veggie Juice

Prep time: 10 minutes | Cook time: 0 minutes | Serves 2

2 medium fennel bulbs
1 small stalk celery
1 small carrot
1 medium apple

1. Peel, cut, deseed, and/or chop the ingredients as needed.
2. Place a container under the juicer's spout.
3. Feed the ingredients one at a time, in the order listed, through the juicer.
4. Stir the juice and pour into glasses to serve.

PER SERVING

Calories: 131| Fat: 1g | Protein: 3g | Carbohydrates: 32g | Sugar: 20mg

Juicy Lettuce with Cilantro
Prep time: 10 minutes | Cook time: 0 minutes | Serves 2

2 large stalks celery
1 large carrot
½ romaine lettuce heart
½ medium cucumber
3 sprigs cilantro

1. Peel, cut, deseed, and/or chop the ingredients as needed.
2. Place a container under the juicer's spout.
3. Feed the ingredients one at a time, in the order listed, through the juicer.
4. Stir the juice and pour into glasses to serve.

PER SERVING

Calories: 24| Fat: 0g | Protein: 1g | Carbohydrates: 5g | Sugar: 3mg

Carrot with Gingered Apple and Cabbage
Prep time: 5 minutes | Cook time: 0 minutes | Serves 2

½ head of green cabbage
16 chard leaves
6 carrots
2 apples
2-inch (5 cm) piece of fresh root ginger

1. Peel, cut, deseed, and/or chop the ingredients as needed.
2. Place a container under the juicer's spout.
3. Feed the first four ingredients one at a time, in the order listed, through the juicer.
4. Stir the hempseed into the juice and pour into glasses to serve.

PER SERVING

Calories: 214| Fat: 1g | Protein: 4g | Carbohydrates: 53g | Sugar: 43mg

Juicy Vegetable Delight
Prep time: 5 minutes | Cook time: 0 minutes | Serves 2

6 carrots
4 apples
2-inch (5 cm) piece of fresh root ginger

1. Peel, cut, deseed, and/or chop the ingredients as needed.
2. Place a container under the juicer's spout.
3. Feed the first four ingredients one at a time, in the order listed, through the juicer.
4. Stir the juice and pour into glasses to serve.

PER SERVING

Calories: 264| Fat: 1g | Protein: 3g | Carbohydrates: 58g | Sugar: 43mg

Mint with Apple-Carrot Limeade
Prep time: 5 minutes | Cook time: 0 minutes | Serves 2

8 carrots
2 cucumbers
4 apples
1 lime
large handful of fresh mint
2-inch (5 cm) piece of fresh root ginger

1. Peel, cut, deseed, and/or chop the ingredients as needed.
2. Place a container under the juicer's spout.
3. Feed the first four ingredients one at a time, in the order listed, through the juicer.
4. Stir the juice and pour into glasses to serve.

PER SERVING

Calories: 104| Fat: 0g | Protein: 2g | Carbohydrates: 27g | Sugar: 2mg

Kale-Packed Juice
Prep time: 5 minutes | Cook time: 0 minutes | Serves 2

10 kale leaves
2 cucumbers
6 celery sticks
2 pears

1. Peel, cut, deseed, and/or chop the ingredients as needed.
2. Place a container under the juicer's spout.
3. Feed the first four ingredients one at a time, in the order listed, through the juicer.
4. Stir the juice and pour into glasses to serve.

PER SERVING

Calories: 24| Fat: 0g | Protein: 1g | Carbohydrates: 4g | Sugar: 3mg

Juicy Celery and Pear Veggie Juice
Prep time: 5 minutes | Cook time: 0 minutes | Serves 1

3 celery roots
2 pears

1. Peel, cut, deseed, and/or chop the ingredients as needed.
2. Place a container under the juicer's spout.
3. Feed the ingredients in the order listed, through the juicer.
4. Stir the juice and pour into glasses to serve.

PER SERVING

Calories: 57| Fat: 0g | Protein: 1g | Carbohydrates: 15g | Sugar: 10mg

Carrot Juice with Ginger Threads
Prep time: 5 minutes | Cook time: 0 minutes | Serves 2

8 large carrots
2 tablespoons of sugar
Salt (optional)
½ inch piece of fresh ginger

1. Wash the carrots and ginger in cold running water.
2. Cut them into slices and place in a blender.
3. Add sugar and salt to it and mix.
4. Strain the mixture using a fine mesh and fill in a jug.
5. Stir the mixture. Either serve it chill or have it as it is.
6. You can add a few threads of ginger on top of the glasses to make it look more tempting.
7. Enjoy!

PER SERVING

Calories: 149 | Fat: 1g | Protein: 3g | Carbohydrates: 36g | Sugar: 21mg

Cool cucumber juice for summer
Prep time: 5 minutes | Cook time: 0 minutes | Serves 2

3 fresh cucumbers
½ cup Fresh lemon juice
½ cup of white sugar
Some water (about a cup)

1. Take the fresh cucumbers. Now peel of their skin and chop them into pieces.
2. Take about half a cup of fresh lemon juice. Place them in a blender and add ½ a cup of white sugar and water (according to how much you want to dilute).
3. Now blend them together and collect the juice.
4. Pour this fresh juice into glasses and serve this delicious cucumber juice topped with some mint leaves.
5. Enjoy!

PER SERVING

Calories: 160 | Fat: 10g | Protein: 3g | Carbohydrates: 17g | Sugar: 11mg

Turnip Fennel Juice
Prep time: 8 minutes | Cook time: 0 minutes | Serves 2
½ Turnip raw/mashed
1 Apple raw
3 Carrots medium raw
¼ Fennel bulb medium raw

1. With the help of a power juicer, convert the above ingredients into juice. If the turnip is highly waxed, then remove the outer skin before introducing it into the juicer.
2. Serve with some ice cubes.
3. Enjoy!

PER SERVING

Calories: 102 | Fat: 05g | Protein: 2g | Carbohydrates: 25g | Sugar: 16mg

Colorful healthy mixed juice
Prep time: 10 minutes | Cook time: 0 minutes | Serves 2

4 fresh lemons
4 baby carrots
4 fresh apples
2 fresh beets
A bunch Cilantro
¼ cup Collard greens
5-6 Kale leaves

1. Take the lemons, peel off the skin and cut into quarters.
2. Then peel the skin off the carrots and chop.
3. Now, take the fresh apples and cut them into quarters.
4. Take the fresh beets and trim and then chop into pieces.
5. Place all the ingredients in a blender and blend together until smooth.
6. Now, collect the juice in a large container.
7. Serve topped with some ice cubes.
8. Enjoy!

PER SERVING

Calories: 261 | Fat: 1g | Protein: 3.5g | Carbohydrates: 68g | Sugar: 47mg

Cool cucumber with avocado juice
Prep time: 8 minutes | Cook time: 0 minutes | Serves 2

3 fresh cucumbers
½ cup Fresh lemon juice
1 Fresh avocado
½ a cup of white sugar
Some water (about a cup)

1. Take the fresh cucumbers. Now peel of their skin and chop them into pieces.
2. Take about half a cup of fresh lemon juice. Deseed the avocado and take its flesh.
3. Place them in a blender and add ½ a cup of white sugar and water.
4. Now blend them together. Pour the fresh juice into glasses and serve this delicious cucumber juice, which can be prepared in less than 15 minutes.
5. Enjoy!

PER SERVING

Calories: 308 | Fat: 15g | Protein: 4g | Carbohydrates: 44g | Sugar: 31mg

Parsley Energy Explosion

Prep time: 5 minutes | Cook time: 0 minutes | Serves 2

1 large bunch Parsley
1 Apple raw
2 Carrots raw
1 Celery raw

1. You will require a good juicer. If u have a centrifugal juicer, then push the parsley into the juicer with celery or carrots to get a good yield.
2. The apple should be introduced to the juicer at the last and hence obtain all the nutrients.
3. Serve topped with some ice cubes.
4. Enjoy!

PER SERVING

Calories: 73 | Fat: 0.3g | Protein: 1g | Carbohydrates: 19g | Sugar: 12mg

Eggplant Carrot Juice Recipe

Prep time: 5 minutes | Cook time: 0 minutes | Serves 2

1 Eggplant raw
3 Carrots raw
2 Apples raw
1 Celery stalk raw

1. Juice up the whole eggplant with the skin and the seeds.
2. Then juice up the other ingredients and pour it into a glass and serve.
3. Enjoy!

PER SERVING

Calories: 202 | Fat: 1g | Protein: 4g | Carbohydrates: 50g | Sugar: 33mg

Tummy Saver Cabbage Juice

Prep time: 6 minutes | Cook time: 0 minutes | Serves 2

½ Head of cabbage raw
2 Celery stalks raw
2 Carrots raw
2 Apples raw

1. After washing, push the vegetables into a power juicer and prepare the juice.
2. Pour it into a glass and serve. Make sure to drink it soon after juicing within a couple of minutes.
3. Enjoy!

PER SERVING

Calories: 166 | Fat: 1g | Protein: 3g | Carbohydrates: 42g | Sugar: 27mg

Savory Satisfying Salad Juice

Prep time: 10 minutes | Cook time: 0 minutes | Serves 2

1 handful Spinach
3 medium sized Tomatoes
2 whole Scallions
2 Celery sticks
2 large Carrots
1 Red pepper (capsicum)
1 teaspoon Olive oil (cold-pressed)
Pepper and sea salt to taste

1. Wash all the ingredients under running water. De-seed capsicum thoroughly; chop all the components as per size fitting to juicer jar.
2. Combine all the ingredients and juice until smooth.
3. Lastly add olive oil and season with sea salt and pepper if desired. Green or yellow bell pepper can also be taken in place of red bell pepper.
4. Enjoy!

PER SERVING

Calories: 105 | Fat: 3g | Protein: 4g | Carbohydrates: 19g | Sugar: 11mg

Chapter 6
Green Juices

Gingered Celery and Spinach Green Juice

Prep time: 10 minutes | Cook time: 0 minutes | Serves 1

2 handfuls of spinach
2 granny smith apples
1 pear, pitted
1 fennel
1 mango
1 celery stalk
½ thumb size piece of ginger

1. Wash all ingredients and process through a juicer.
2. Pour the extracted juice into a glass, stir well and drink immediately.

PER SERVING

Calories: 98| Fat: 0g | Protein: 1g | Carbohydrates: 23g | Sugar: 16mg

Lemony Apple and Spinach Green Juice

Prep time: 5 minutes | Cook time: 0 minutes | Serves 1

2 apples
1 bunch spinach
½ lemon, peeled

1. Wash the spinach, apples and lemon and cut into chunks.
2. Add to a juicer and process.
3. Pour into a glass and drink immediately.

PER SERVING

Calories: 273| Fat: 2g | Protein: 11g | Carbohydrates: 64g | Sugar: 40mg

Beet with Citrus Veggie Green Juice

Prep time: 5 minutes | Cook time: 0 minutes | Serves 1

1 medium beet, peeled
2 leaves of red cabbage
3 medium carrots
½ lemon, peeled
1 orange, peeled
½ pineapple
2 handfuls of spinach

1. Peel the pineapple, beet, orange and citrus and process through a juicer along with spinach, carrots, and cabbage leaves.
2. Pour the extracted juice into a glass and enjoy.

PER SERVING

Calories: 57| Fat: 0g | Protein: 1g | Carbohydrates: 15g | Sugar: 10mg

Parsley with Radish Green Juice

Prep time: 5 minutes | Cook time: 0 minutes | Serves 1

2 stalks of celery
½ lemon
½ bunch of kale
3-inch chunk of daikon radish
1 small cucumber
½ bunch of spinach
A few sprigs of cilantro or flat leaf parsley

1. Pass the celery, kale, radish, cucumber, spinach, lemon, and cilantro through a juicer.
2. If the juice is too strong for you, add a pear or apple to sweeten it.

PER SERVING

Calories: 128| Fat: 1g | Protein: 6g | Carbohydrates: 26g | Sugar: 15mg

Simple Lemony Celery Green Juice

Prep time: 5 minutes | Cook time: 0 minutes | Serves 1

1 bunch kale
1 bunch celery
1 lemon

1. Wash the celery kale and lemon and run through a juicer.
2. Drink immediately.

PER SERVING

Calories: 23| Fat: 0g | Protein: 1g | Carbohydrates: 5g | Sugar: 1mg

Kale with Healthy Apples Green Juice

Prep time: 5 minutes | Cook time: 0 minutes | Serves 1

2 cups of Swiss chard
1 cup of kale
2 carrots
2 celery stalks
2 apples

1. Add the greens to a juicer and process along with apples, carrots, and celery stalks.
2. Pour the juice into a glass and drink immediately.

PER SERVING

Calories: 133| Fat: 0g | Protein: 2g | Carbohydrates: 33g | Sugar: 1mg

Gingered Celery with Green Cabbage Juice

Prep time: 5 minutes | Cook time: 0 minutes | Serves 1

½ head green or Napa cabbage
1 bunch dandelion greens
½ bunch celery
½ lemon, unpeeled
1-inch knob of fresh ginger root

1. Process the cabbage, celery, dandelion greens, lemon, and ginger through a juicer.
2. Add little honey to provide the juice some sweetness.

PER SERVING

Calories: 47| Fat: 0g | Protein: 2g | Carbohydrates: 11g | Sugar: 6mg

Carrot with Ginger Green Power Juice

Prep time: 5 minutes | Cook time: 0 minutes | Serves 1

2 stalks celery
2 small apples
2 carrots
5 small radishes
1 small piece ginger
1 cup spinach

1. Wash the apples, carrots, radishes, spinach and cut into chunks.
2. Add to a juicer along with a piece of ginger.
3. Pour the extracted juice into a glass, stir well and drink.

PER SERVING

Calories: 109| Fat: 27g | Protein: 0g | Carbohydrates: 1g | Sugar: 19mg

Herb with Super Green Juice

Prep time: 5 minutes | Cook time: 0 minutes | Serves 1

2 leaves Swiss chard
1 cup kale
½ cup parsley
½ small beet
½ cup pineapple, chipped
2 medium green apples, chopped
1 sprig fresh mint
½ medium lemon, peeled

1. Wash the herbs under running water. Make sure not to leave dirt on the leaves. Place in a juicer.
2. Add the beet, pineapple, green apples and lemon and process.
3. Pour into a tall glass and enjoy.

PER SERVING

Calories: 243| Fat: 3g | Protein: 2g | Carbohydrates: 53g | Sugar: 44mg

Spinach with Fruity Green Juice

Prep time: 5 minutes | Cook time: 0 minutes | Serves 2

1 bunch spinach leaves
1 medium apple
1 medium pear
1 medium navel orange

1. Peel, cut, deseed, and/or chop the ingredients as needed.
2. Place a container under the juicer's spout.
3. Feed the ingredients one at a time, in the order listed, through the juicer.
4. Stir the juice and pour into glasses to serve.

PER SERVING

Calories: 86| Fat: 0g | Protein: 6g | Carbohydrates: 19g | Sugar: 10mg

Spinach with Kale Tango Green Juice

Prep time: 5 minutes | Cook time: 0 minutes | Serves 2

4 large kale leaves
3 large stalks celery
1 ripe mango
1 small bunch spinach leaves

1. Peel, cut, deseed, and/or chop the ingredients as needed.
2. Place a container under the juicer's spout.
3. Feed the ingredients one at a time, in the order listed, through the juicer.
4. Stir the juice and pour into glasses to serve.

PER SERVING

Calories: 86 Fat: 1g | Protein: 10g | Carbohydrates: 13g | Sugar: 2mg

Royal Broccoli with Zucchini Green Juice

Prep time: 5 minutes | Cook time: 0 minutes | Serves 1

½ head broccoli
4 leaves kale
½ green bell pepper
1 zucchini, peeled
1 green apple

1. Wash the pepper, broccoli, zucchini, kale, and apple and cut into chunks.
2. Then pass all ingredients through a juicer.
3. Pour the juice into a glass and drink immediately.

PER SERVING

Calories: 53| Fat: 0g | Protein: 1g | Carbohydrates: 14g | Sugar: 10mg

Asparagus with Honeydew Green Lemonade
Prep time: 5 minutes | Cook time: 0 minutes | Serves 2

1 small honeydew melon
1 bunch asparagus
1 medium pear
1 lemon

1. Peel, cut, deseed, and/or chop the ingredients as needed.
2. Place a container under the juicer's spout.
3. Feed the ingredients one at a time, in the order listed, through the juicer.
4. Stir the juice and pour into glasses to serve.

PER SERVING

Calories: 34| Fat: 0g | Protein: 0g | Carbohydrates: 9g | Sugar: 6mg

Simple Celery Green Juice
Prep time: 5 minutes | Cook time: 0 minutes | Serves 1

4 romaine lettuce leaves
4 celery ribs
1 green apple

1. Wash all the ingredients.
2. Trim the ends from the celery, then and cut into 4-inch pieces.
3. Remove the apple core and discard. Cut the apple into quarters, leaving the peel intact.
4. Place a pitcher under the juicer's spout to collect the juice.
5. Feed each ingredient through the juicer's intake tube in the order listed.
6. When the juice stops flowing, remove the pitcher and stir the juice.
7. Serve immediately.

PER SERVING

Calories: 73| Fat: 1g | Protein: 2g | Carbohydrates: 23g | Sugar: 8mg

Lemony Kale and Celery Green Juice
Prep time: 5 minutes | Cook time: 0 minutes | Serves 2

2 green apples, halved
4 stalks celery
1 cucumber, pealed
6 romaine leaves
5 kale leaves
1 lemon, peeled

1. Thoroughly wash all the ingredients under running cold water and run the through a juicer.
2. Pour the juice into 2 glasses and serve with ice.

PER SERVING

Calories: 117| Fat: 0g | Protein: 1g | Carbohydrates: 30g | Sugar: 21mg

Lemony Cucumber Green Juice
Prep time: 5 minutes | Cook time: 0 minutes | Serves 1

1 cup spinach
4 celery ribs
1 green apple
1 cucumber
½ lemon

1. Wash all the ingredients.
2. Trim the ends from the celery and cucumber, then cut into 4-inch pieces.
3. Remove the apple core and discard. Cut the apple into quarters, leaving the peel intact.
4. Peel the lemon and cut into quarters.
5. Place a pitcher under the juicer's spout to collect the juice.
6. Feed each ingredient through the juicer's intake tube in the order listed.
7. When the juice stops flowing, remove the pitcher and stir the juice.
8. Serve immediately.

PER SERVING

Calories: 102| Fat: 1g | Protein: 3g | Carbohydrates: 32g | Sugar: 19mg

Broccoli with Mellow Celery
Prep time: 5 minutes | Cook time: 0 minutes | Serves 1

4 celery ribs
1 cucumber
2 cups broccoli
½ lemon

1. Wash all the ingredients.
2. Trim the ends from the celery and cucumber, then cut into 4-inch pieces.
3. Remove the stalk from the broccoli crown with a knife and discard or save to juice later. Cut the crown into small florets.
4. Peel the lemon and cut into quarters.
5. Place a pitcher under the juicer's spout to collect the juice.
6. Feed each ingredient through the juicer's intake tube in the order listed.
7. When the juice stops flowing, remove the pitcher and stir the juice.
8. Serve immediately.

PER SERVING

Calories: 148| Fat: 2g | Protein: 14g | Carbohydrates: 41g | Sugar: 13mg

Parsley with Lettuce Special

Prep time: 5 minutes | Cook time: 0 minutes | Serves 1

2 cups romaine lettuce (about 4 leaves)
2 tablespoons parsley leaves
½ green apple
½ beet
1 lemon

1. Wash all the ingredients.
2. Remove the apple core and discard. Cut the apple into quarters, leaving the peel intact.
3. Remove any greens from the beet and save for juicing later. Cut the beet into quarters.
4. Peel the lemon and cut into quarters.
5. Place a pitcher under the juicer's spout to collect the juice.
6. Feed each ingredient through the juicer's intake tube in the order listed.
7. When the juice stops flowing, remove the pitcher and stir the juice.
8. Serve immediately.

PER SERVING

Calories: 63| Fat: 1g | Protein: 3g | Carbohydrates: 21g | Sugar: 12mg

Minty Chia Green Bliss

Prep time: 5 minutes | Cook time: 0 minutes | Serves 1

3 cups spinach
10 mint leaves
1 green apple
1 teaspoon chia seeds

1. Wash all the spinach, mint leaves, and apple.
2. Remove the apple core and discard. Cut the apple into quarters, leaving the peel intact.
3. Place a pitcher under the juicer's spout to collect the juice.
4. Feed the first three ingredients through the juicer's intake tube in the order listed.
5. When the juice stops flowing, remove the pitcher, add the chia seeds, stir the juice, and let sit for five minutes.
6. Serve immediately.

PER SERVING

Calories: 74| Fat: 1g | Protein: 3g | Carbohydrates: 21g | Sugar: 13mg

Blue Pear with Green Lemonade

Prep time: 5 minutes | Cook time: 0 minutes | Serves 1

4 kale leaves
1 cucumber
1 pear
½ cup blueberries
1 lemon

1. Wash all the ingredients.
2. Trim the ends from the cucumber, then cut into 4-inch pieces.
3. Cut the pear into quarters, removing the seeds but leaving the peel intact.
4. Peel the lemon and cut into quarters.
5. Place a pitcher under the juicer's spout to collect the juice.
6. Feed each ingredient through the juicer's intake tube in the order listed.
7. When the juice stops flowing, remove the pitcher and stir the juice.
8. Serve immediately.

PER SERVING

Calories: 187| Fat: 2g | Protein: 8g | Carbohydrates: 61g | Sugar: 30mg

Arugula Green Juice

Prep time: 5 minutes | Cook time: 0 minutes | Serves 1

1 romaine lettuce heart
½ cup arugula
2 pears
½ lemon

1. Wash all the ingredients.
2. Cut the pears into quarters, removing the seeds but leaving the peel intact.
3. Peel the lemon and cut into quarters.
4. Place a pitcher under the juicer's spout to collect the juice.
5. Feed each ingredient through the juicer's intake tube in the order listed.
6. When the juice stops flowing, remove the pitcher and stir the juice.
7. Serve immediately.

PER SERVING

Calories: 181| Fat: 1g | Protein: 5g | Carbohydrates: 63g | Sugar: 35mg

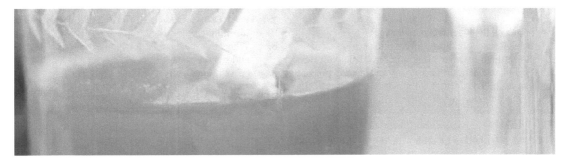

Limey Green Juice with Red Apples
Prep time: 5 minutes | Cook time: 0 minutes | Serves 2

1 lime
4 kale leaves
1/3 pineapple
2 red apples
1-inch knob of ginger
A handful Italian parsley

1. Wash the kale, parsley, lime, and apples. Remove the zest of the lime. Cut the apples into chunks and run through a juicer, alternating with the remaining ingredients.
2. Apples will ease the process by pushing down the other ingredients.
3. Pour the fresh juice into a tall glass and drink immediately.

PER SERVING

Calories: 100| Fat: 0g | Protein: 1g | Carbohydrates: 27g | Sugar: 19mg

Gingered Carrot with Oregano Green Juice
Prep time: 5 minutes | Cook time: 0 minutes | Serves 1

1 to 2 stalks celery
1 green apple, seeds removed
1 large orange, peeled
1 small bunch organic kale
2 small handfuls spinach
1-inch piece of fresh ginger
1 large carrot
Freshly squeezed lemon juice to taste

1. Thoroughly wash the fruits and vegetables.
2. Run through a juicer and pour into a tall glass.
3. Stir in the freshly squeezed lemon juice to your taste, add 2 to 3 ice cubes and enjoy.

PER SERVING

Calories: 251| Fat: 9g | Protein: 8g | Carbohydrates: 36g | Sugar: 21mg

Chilled Peachy Green Juice
Prep time: 5 minutes | Cook time: 0 minutes | Serves 2

2 Peaches
2 Limes
4 to 5 cups Swiss chard stalks (silver beet is preferable)

1. Wash all the ingredients under water.
2. Peel peaches and lime and cut into slices as desired.
3. Juice them together using a juicer. Made with three ingredients only, the juice is easy and quick to prepare.
4. Serve chilled.
5. Enjoy!

PER SERVING

Calories: 365 | Fat: 1g | Protein: 5g | Carbohydrates: 92g | Sugar: 75mg

Spicy Carrot with Vegetable Green Juice
Prep time: 5 minutes | Cook time: 0 minutes | Serves 1

2 medium tomatoes
1 cucumber
1 cup spinach
1 cup cabbage
½ red bell pepper
2 celery ribs
2 carrots
1 green onion

1. Wash all the ingredients.
2. Remove stems from the tomatoes and cut into quarters.
3. Trim the ends from the cucumber, celery, carrots, and green onion, then cut into 4-inch pieces.
4. Cut cabbage in half, then slice or chop into smaller pieces.
5. Remove the stem and seeds from the bell pepper. Cut into small pieces.
6. Place a pitcher under the juicer's spout to collect the juice.
7. Feed each ingredient through the juicer's intake tube in the order listed.
8. When the juice stops flowing, remove the pitcher and stir the juice.
9. Serve immediately.

PER SERVING

Calories: 104| Fat: 1g | Protein: 6g | Carbohydrates: 30g | Sugar: 16mg

Spiced Lemon with Lettuce Green Juice
Prep time: 5 minutes | Cook time: 0 minutes | Serves 1

3 carrots
6 romaine lettuce leaves
2 medium tomatoes
2 green onions
½ green bell pepper
¼ cup parsley
½ lemon

1. Wash all the ingredients.
2. Trim the ends from carrots and green onions, then cut into 4-inch pieces.
3. Remove the stems from the tomatoes and cut into quarters.
4. Remove the stem and seeds from the bell pepper. Cut into small pieces.
5. Peel the lemon half and cut into quarters.
6. Place a pitcher under the juicer's spout to collect the juice.
7. Feed each ingredient through the juicer's intake tube in the order listed.
8. When the juice stops flowing, remove the pitcher and stir the juice.
9. Serve immediately.

PER SERVING

Calories: 89| Fat: 1g | Protein: 5g | Carbohydrates: 28g | Sugar: 14mg

Lemony Parsley with Green Turbo

Prep time: 5 minutes | Cook time: 0 minutes | Serves 1

½ cup spinach
3 kale leaves
2 green apples
2 celery ribs
½ cup parsley
1 cucumber
½ lemon
Fresh ginger root

1. Wash all the ingredients.
2. Remove the apple core and discard. Cut the apples into quarters, leaving the peel intact.
3. Trim the ends from the celery and cucumber, then cut into 4-inch pieces.
4. Peel the lemon half and cut into quarters.
5. Slice off a ½-inch piece of fresh ginger root.
6. Place a pitcher under the juicer's spout to collect the juice.
7. Feed each ingredient through the juicer's intake tube in the order listed.
8. When the juice stops flowing, remove the pitcher and stir the juice.
9. Serve immediately.

PER SERVING

Calories: 173| Fat: 2g | Protein: 7g | Carbohydrates: 53g | Sugar: 29mg

Lettuce with Sprouts Green Juice

Prep time: 5 minutes | Cook time: 0 minutes | Serves 1

4 celery ribs
1 cucumber
8 lettuce leaves
½ cup alfalfa sprouts

1. Wash all the ingredients.
2. Trim the ends from the celery and cucumber, then cut into 4-inch pieces.
3. Place a pitcher under the juicer's spout to collect the juice.
4. Feed each ingredient through the juicer's intake tube in the order listed.
5. When the juice stops flowing, remove the pitcher and stir the juice.
6. Serve immediately.

PER SERVING

Calories: 55| Fat: 1g | Protein: 5g | Carbohydrates: 16g | Sugar: 7mg

Cucumber with Pear Green Juice

Prep time: 10 minutes | Cook time: 0 minutes | Serves 1

1 cup spinach
2 cups green beans
1 cucumber
½ pear
½ lemon

1. Wash all the ingredients.
2. Trim the ends from the green beans and cucumber, then cut into 4-inch pieces.
3. Cut the pear into quarters, removing the core and seeds, but leaving the peel intact.
4. Peel the lemon half and cut into quarters.
5. Place a pitcher under the juicer's spout to collect the juice.
6. Feed each ingredient through the juicer's intake tube in the order listed.
7. When the juice stops flowing, remove the pitcher and stir the juice.
8. Serve immediately.

PER SERVING

Calories: 102| Fat: 1g | Protein: 6g | Carbohydrates: 34g | Sugar: 16mg

Watermelon with Kale Green Juice

Prep time: 5 minutes | Cook time: 0 minutes | Serves 1

1½ cups watermelon
4 kale leaves
½ lime
2 celery ribs

1. Wash the kale, lime, and celery.
2. Cut the watermelon into quarters. Remove the rind and discard. Cut the watermelon into smaller pieces.
3. Trim the ends from the celery, then cut into 4-inch pieces.
4. Peel the lime half and cut into quarters.
5. Place a pitcher under the juicer's spout to collect the juice.
6. Feed each ingredient through the juicer's intake tube in the order listed.
7. When the juice stops flowing, remove the pitcher and stir the juice.
8. Serve immediately.

PER SERVING

Calories: 90| Fat: 1g | Protein: 6g | Carbohydrates: 24g | Sugar: 13mg

Broccoli Watercress Green Juice

Prep time: 5 minutes | Cook time: 0 minutes | Serves 1

2 cups spinach
1 cup clover sprouts
1 cup watercress
2 green apples
2 cups broccoli

1. Wash all the ingredients.
2. Remove the apple cores and discard. Cut the apples into quarters, leaving the peel intact.
3. Remove the stalk from the broccoli crown with a knife and discard or save to juice later. Cut the crown into small florets.
4. Place a pitcher under the juicer's spout to collect the juice.
5. Feed each ingredient through the juicer's intake tube in the order listed.
6. When the juice stops flowing, remove the pitcher and stir the juice.
7. Serve immediately.

PER SERVING

Calories: 114| Fat: 1g | Protein: 5g | Carbohydrates: 34g | Sugar: 23mg

Gingered Green Juice with Lemon

Prep time: 15 minutes | Cook time: 0 minutes | Serves 2

2 Fresh green apples cut into halves
2 Fresh celery stalks with their leaves removed
1 Fresh cucumber, skin peeled off
4-5 Fresh kale leaves
½ a fresh lemon (peel off the skin)
A small piece of fresh ginger

1. Take all the fresh ingredients. Peel and chop them coarsely.
2. Now, put all these ingredients in a juicer. Extract the green juice and keep it in a large container.
3. Then serve in glasses and top the glasses with some more grated ginger and a bit of lime juice.
4. Enjoy!

PER SERVING

Calories: 154 | Fat: 3g | Protein: 7g | Carbohydrates: 28g | Sugar: 21mg

Banana with Garden Green Drink

Prep time: 5 minutes | Cook time: 0 minutes | Serves 1

1 Thai Coconut
1 handful of spinach
1 handful of green kale
½ banana

1. Take all ingredients except green kale.
2. Blend, add some water in it and blend again. Your juice is ready.
3. Serve topped with some kale leaves.
4. Enjoy!

PER SERVING

Calories: 117 | Fat: 1g | Protein: 5g | Carbohydrates: 25g | Sugar: 13mg

Green Powerhouse Juice

Prep time: 15 minutes | Cook time: 0 minutes | Serves 2

4 Fresh beet roots
2 Fresh celery stalks with their leaves removed
1 fresh cucumber, skin peeled off
1 bunch Fresh spinach
½ a fresh lemon (peel off the skin)
A small piece of fresh ginger

1. Take all the fresh ingredients. Peel and chop them into bite sized pieces. Now put all these ingredients in a juicer.
2. Extract the green juice and keep it in a large container.
3. Pour into glasses and some more grated ginger, a bit of lime juice and a slice of cucumber.
4. Serve immediately.
5. Enjoy!

PER SERVING

Calories: 165 | Fat: 3.5g | Protein: 13g | Carbohydrates: 24g | Sugar: 13mg

Raw Popeye's Green Juice

Prep time: 10 minutes | Cook time: 0 minutes | Serves 2

1 large handful Spinach leaves
2 kale leaves raw
1 beet with top raw (without skin)
1 apple raw
2 celery stalks raw
2 teaspoons Blackstrap molasses

1. Wash the vegetables before introducing it into the juicer. Ensure to leave the skin on beet before juicing.
2. Add all the ingredients and when the juice is ready pour it into a glass and serve.
3. Enjoy!

PER SERVING

Calories: 84 | Fat: 0.3g | Protein: 1g | Carbohydrates: 21g | Sugar: 17mg

Ginegery Greens & Peach Juice

Prep time: 10 minutes | Cook time: 0 minutes | Serves 2

1 Peach
5-6 Carrots
½ Lemon
1 inch Ginger
1 handful Frisee
1 handful Arugula

1. Wash all the ingredients properly and prepare them to be introduced into the juicer.
2. Add the ingredients through the juicer and prepare the juice. After preparing, pour it into a glass and serve.
3. Enjoy!

PER SERVING

Calories: 105 | Fat: 1g | Protein: 3g | Carbohydrates: 25g | Sugar: 15mg

Gingery Pine-Lime Green Juice

Prep time: 8 minutes | Cook time: 0 minutes | Serves 2

¼ part Pineapple
1 bunch Spinach
1 small Baby Bok Choy
2 cups Celery stalks
1 Lime
1 inch Ginger

1. Peel the lime and pineapple. Wash under water properly. Chop ingredients into slices as per requirements.
2. Blend them together in a juicer and juice until smooth. Apple or pear can be a traditional replacement in place of pineapple and kale can go better replacing spinach. Serve chilled.
3. Enjoy!

PER SERVING

Calories: 67 | Fat: 1g | Protein: 6g | Carbohydrates: 13g | Sugar: 4mg

Minty Low Sugar Green Juice

Prep time: 10 minutes | Cook time: 0 minutes | Serves 2

½ Green apple
3 Kale leaves
Mint leaves with stems 8 pcs
3 Limes, peeled
1 ¼ Cucumbers, peeled
2 cups Spinach, chopped

1. Wash all the ingredients. Taste cucumber to avoid any bitter taste. Peeling lime is optional for providing zestier taste.
2. Combine all ingredients together and blend them in juicer until smooth. You can use cabbage in place of chard and basil in place of mint.
3. Enjoy!

PER SERVING

Calories: 69 | Fat: 1g | Protein: 3g | Carbohydrates: 17g | Sugar: 8mg

Lovey Dovey Green Juice

Prep time: 10 minutes | Cook time: 0 minutes | Serves 2

½ Lemon, peeled
½ cup Cilantro leaves (with stems)
1 Kale leaf (with stem)
1 handful Spinach leaves
1 Carrot, scrubbed with ends trimmed
½ Beet, scrubbed
½ Cucumber, unpeeled with ends trimmed
3 Celery stalks (with leaves)

1. Wash all the ingredients properly before introducing into the juicer. Peel off the lemon and the beet.
2. Trim the ends of the carrots and the cucumber and chop it into pieces so that they enter the mouth of the juicer.
3. After preparing the juice, pour it into a glass put some ice cubes or put it into refrigerator till its chilled and then serve.
4. Enjoy!

PER SERVING

Calories: 34 | Fat: 0.3g | Protein: 1.5g | Carbohydrates: 7g | Sugar: 4mg

Carroty Green Juice Detoxifier

Prep time: 10 minutes | Cook time: 0 minutes | Serves 2

5 stalks of fresh spinach, freshly cleaned and cut into pieces.
3 carrots, peeled and cut into pieces.
1 sweet red apple, unpeeled and cut into pieces
1 broccoli, its spear, and head

1. Blend all the ingredients together in the juicer. But the grinding should be done in a slow process by adding little water.
2. Pour it in a glass and garnish with a carrot. It must be served at room temperature. You can have it regularly, but to get the best results, it is recommended to drink at least four times a week.
3. Enjoy!

PER SERVING

Calories: 93 | Fat: 0.4g | Protein: 1.4g | Carbohydrates: 22g | Sugar: 14mg

Simple Homemade Green Juice

Prep time: 10 minutes | Cook time: 0 minutes | Serves 2

3 Apples medium
¼ Ginger Root
½ Lemon (with rind)
1 Large Orange (peeled)
5 Spinach
4 Celery stalk
½ Lemon (with rind)

1. You don't have to peel the lemon, but make sure you peel the orange. The orange's skin is very bitter and can ruin the flavor.
2. Process all ingredients in a juicer, shake or stir and serve.
3. Enjoy!

PER SERVING

Calories: 202 | Fat: 1g | Protein: 3g | Carbohydrates: 52g | Sugar: 38mg

Lemony Green Aid

Prep time: 10 minutes | Cook time: 0 minutes | Serves 2

4 Apples (granny smith)
3 Celery stalk
2 Kales
1 Lemon (peeled)
4 cups Spinach

1. All the ingredients like celery stalk, spinach, lemon are put in a container.
2. Then all ingredients are processed well in a juicer.
3. Let them to blend all properly. Shake or stir and serve.
4. Enjoy!

PER SERVING

Calories: 214 | Fat: 1g | Protein: 3g | Carbohydrates: 55g | Sugar: 39mg

Spinach with Orange Green Recipe

Prep time: 5 minutes | Cook time: 0 minutes | Serves 2

2 Fresh Oranges
2 Large frozen bananas
1 Handful of baby spinach

1. First you collect all the fresh ingredients and clean all of them with plain water. At first the oranges are placed in the juicer to extract the juice from it.
2. Blend the bananas in the blender until smooth.
3. Add the orange juice into the blender.
4. Add some of the spinach and blend again. Serve topped with some ice cubes and pieces of torn spinach.
5. Enjoy!

PER SERVING

Calories: 227 | Fat: 1g | Protein: 4g | Carbohydrates: 57g | Sugar: 17mg

Lettuce with Gingery Green Juice

Prep time: 10 minutes | Cook time: 0 minutes | Serves 1

2 apples
½ cucumber
½ lemon, peeled
½ cup kale
½ cup spinach
¼ bunch celery
¼ bulb fennel
1-inch piece ginger
¼ head romaine lettuce

1. Take all ingredients except green kale.
2. Blend, add some water in it and blend again. Your juice is ready.
3. Serve topped with some kale leaves.
4. Enjoy!

PER SERVING

Calories: 260 | Fat: 1g | Protein: 5g | Carbohydrates: 66g | Sugar: 46g

Chapter 7
Weight Loss Juices

Jalapeño with Cilantro Juice

Prep time: 5 minutes | Cook time: 0 minutes | Serves 1

1 orange
¼ fresh pineapple
½ handful cilantro
½ small jalapeno, seeded

1. Peel the pineapple and orange and process through a juicer along with jalapeno and cilantro.
2. Pour the juice into a glass and enjoy.

PER SERVING

Calories: 71| Fat: 0g | Protein: 1g | Carbohydrates: 20g | Sugar: 15mg

Grapy Weight Loss Juice

Prep time: 5 minutes | Cook time: 0 minutes | Serves 1

1 ruby grapefruit
1 orange
2 carrots
½-inch (1 cm) piece of ginger

1. Wash and peel all ingredients.
2. Pass through a juicer and drink immediately.

PER SERVING

Calories: 25| Fat: 0g | Protein: 0g | Carbohydrates: 6g | Sugar: 3mg

Icy Orange Juice with Lemon

Prep time: 5 minutes | Cook time: 0 minutes | Serves 1

½ young cabbage
1 small carrot
3 oranges, peeled
½ lemon juice
a thumb size piece of ginger
Ice cubes

1. Run the carrot, ginger, cabbage, and oranges through a juicer.
2. Pour into a glass, add the lemon juice, stir well, and enjoy.

PER SERVING

Calories: 25| Fat: 0g | Protein: 0g | Carbohydrates: 6g | Sugar: 3mg

Fruity Weight Loss Mixed Juice

Prep time: 5 minutes | Cook time: 0 minutes | Serves 1

4 rounds of pineapple
1 grapefruit (juice of 1 grapefruit)
1 cup of water

1. Peel the pineapple and slice into rounds.
2. Run through a juicer along with the grapefruit. Pour the juice into a tall glass, add 1 cup of water, stir well and drink immediately.

PER SERVING

Calories: 84| Fat: 0g | Protein: 2g | Carbohydrates: 21g | Sugar: 18mg

Celery Avocado Mix with Ice

Prep time: 5 minutes | Cook time: 0 minutes | Serves 1

½ ripe avocado
½ small pineapple
2 apples, cored, quartered
½ stick celery
1 small handful of spinach leaves
1 small piece of peeled lime
½ of medium cucumber
Ice cubes

1. Core the apples and cut into quarters.
2. Run through a juicer along with the cucumber, lime, spinach, pineapple, and celery.
3. Peel the avocado and put in a blender. Add a couple of ice cubes and pulse for 20 to 30 seconds until smooth.
4. In a glass, combine the avocado mixture with the extracted juice, stir well and drink immediately.

PER SERVING

Calories: 187| Fat: 8g | Protein: 2g | Carbohydrates: 32g | Sugar: 20mg

Limey Weight Loss Mix

Prep time: 5 minutes | Cook time: 0 minutes | Serves 1

2 pink grapefruits
1 lime

1. Using a juicer or a citrus press, juice the grapefruits and lime.
2. Pour into a glass over ice and drink immediately.

PER SERVING

Calories: 87| Fat: 0g | Protein: 2g | Carbohydrates: 83g | Sugar: 22mg

Lemony Lettuce with Lime and Berries

Prep time: 5 minutes | Cook time: 0 minutes | Serves 2

1 cucumber
1 head romaine lettuce
1 lemon, peeled
1 lime, peeled
1 orange, peeled
2 apples
1 pint of berries (blackberries, raspberries)
4 large carrots

1. Run the cucumber, lime, lemon, orange, carrots, apples, berries, and lettuce through a juicer.
2. Pour into a glass and enjoy.
3. For better results, drink the juice in the morning.

PER SERVING

Calories: 312| Fat: 2g | Protein: 8g | Carbohydrates: 74g | Sugar: 39mg

Weight Loss Detox Green Juice

Prep time: 5 minutes | Cook time: 0 minutes | Serves 2

1 green apple
1 cucumber
2 handfuls of spinach
1 handful of parsley
1 celery stick

1. Pass the cucumber along with spinach, parsley, celery, and apple through a juicer.
2. Pour into a glass over ice and serve immediately.

PER SERVING

Calories: 62| Fat: 0g | Protein: 1g | Carbohydrates: 15g | Sugar: 11mg

Minty Green Juice with Kale and Lime

Prep time: 10 minutes | Cook time: 0 minutes | Serves 2

1 lime, unpeeled
1.5 to 2 cups spinach
8 large kale leaves
12 strawberries
2 Granny Smith apples
A handful of fresh mint

1. Thoroughly wash the kale, spinach, lime, apples, mint, and strawberries.
2. Run all the ingredients through a juicer.
3. Pour the extracted juice into a tall glass over ice and drink immediately.

PER SERVING

Calories: 131| Fat: 0g | Protein: 2g | Carbohydrates: 31g | Sugar: 20mg

Pineapple Mint with Coconut Juice

Prep time: 15 minutes | Cook time: 0 minutes | Serves 1

1 cup pineapple
4 large lettuce leaves
15 mint leaves
½ cup coconut water

1. Wash the lettuce and mint.
2. Trim the ends and skin from the pineapple, then remove the core and discard. Cut pineapple into 1-inch chunks.
3. Place a pitcher under the juicer's spout to collect the juice.
4. Feed the first three ingredients through the juicer's intake tube in the order listed.
5. When the juice stops flowing, remove the pitcher, add the coconut water, and stir.
6. Serve immediately.

PER SERVING

Calories: 71| Fat: 1g | Protein: 2g | Carbohydrates: 21g | Sugar: 14g

Cucumber with Cilantro Mixed Veggie

Prep time: 15 minutes | Cook time: 0 minutes | Serves 1

1 cup pineapple
1 cup spinach
1 cup chopped lettuce leaves
1 cucumber
10 sprigs cilantro

1. Wash all the ingredients except the pineapple.
2. Trim the ends and skin from the pineapple, then remove the core and discard. Cut pineapple into 1-inch chunks.
3. Trim the ends from the cucumber, then cut into 4-inch pieces.
4. Place a pitcher under the juicer's spout to collect the juice.
5. Feed each ingredient through the juicer's intake tube in the order listed.
6. When the juice stops flowing, remove the pitcher and stir the juice.
7. Serve immediately.

PER SERVING

Calories: 87| Fat: 1g | Protein: 3g | Carbohydrates: 25g | Sugar: 15g

Parsley with Green Tea and Orange Juice

Prep time: 20 minutes | Cook time: 0 minutes | Serves 1

¾ cup green tea, cooled
10 dandelion greens
10 parsley sprigs
1 orange

1. Brew the green tea and let cool.
2. Wash the dandelion greens, parsley, and orange.
3. Peel the orange and separate into sections.
4. Place a pitcher under the juicer's spout to collect the juice.
5. Feed the dandelion greens, parsley, and orange through the juicer's intake tube in the order listed.
6. When the juice stops flowing, remove the pitcher, add the green tea to the juice, and stir.
7. Serve immediately.

PER SERVING

Calories: 61| Fat: 1g | Protein: 3g | Carbohydrates: 18g | Sugar: 9g

Apple-Lemon-Cucumber Mixed Juice

Prep time: 20 minutes | Cook time: 0 minutes | Serves 1

½ cup water
1 teaspoon matcha powder
4 green lettuce leaves
½ cucumber
½ lemon
½ green apple

1. Heat the water to 180°F. Whisk in the matcha powder and let cool.
2. Wash the lettuce, cucumber, lemon, and apple.
3. Trim the ends from the cucumber, then cut into 4-inch pieces.
4. Peel the lemon and cut into quarters.
5. Remove the apple core and discard. Cut the apple into quarters, leaving the peel intact.
6. Place a pitcher under the juicer's spout to collect the juice.
7. Feed the lettuce, cucumber, lemon, and apple through the juicer's intake tube in the order listed.
8. When the juice stops flowing, remove the pitcher, add the matcha mixture, and stir.
9. Serve immediately.

PER SERVING

Calories: 63| Fat: 0g | Protein: 1g | Carbohydrates: 20g | Sugar: 13g

Turmeric Spiced Lime Juice

Prep time: 15 minutes | Cook time: 0 minutes | Serves 1

6 kale leaves
2 pears
Fresh turmeric root
½ lime
½ teaspoon ground cinnamon

1. Wash the kale, pears, turmeric root, and lime.
2. Cut the pear into quarters, removing the core and seeds, but leaving the peel intact.
3. Slice off a 2-inch piece of the turmeric root.
4. Peel the lime and cut into quarters.
5. Place a pitcher under the juicer's spout to collect the juice.
6. Feed the first four ingredients through the juicer's intake tube in the order listed.
7. When the juice stops flowing, remove the pitcher, add the cinnamon, and stir the juice.
8. Serve immediately.

PER SERVING

Calories: 194| Fat: 2g | Protein: 8g | Carbohydrates: 58g | Sugar: 28g

Filtered Celery Juice

Prep time: 15 minutes | Cook time: 0 minutes | Serves 1

6 asparagus spears
1 green apple
2 celery ribs
¼ cup filtered water

1. Wash the asparagus, apple, and celery.
2. Trim ½ inch from the bottom of the asparagus, then cut stalks into 4-inch pieces.
3. Remove the apple core and discard. Cut the apple into quarters, leaving the peel intact.
4. Trim the ends from the celery, then cut into 4-inch pieces.
5. Place a pitcher under the juicer's spout to collect the juice.
6. Feed the asparagus, apple, and celery through the juicer's intake tube.
7. When the juice stops flowing, remove the pitcher, add the filtered water, and stir the juice.
8. Serve immediately.

PER SERVING

Calories: 61| Fat: 0g | Protein: 2g | Carbohydrates: 19g | Sugar: 13g

Beet Greens Mixed Juice

Prep time: 15 minutes | Cook time: 0 minutes | Serves 1

1 bunch beet greens (5 to 6 stems)
1 green apple
1 cucumber
2 carrots
1 tomato
Fresh ginger root

1. Remove beet greens from beets.
2. Wash all the ingredients.
3. Remove the apple core and discard. Cut the apple into quarters, leaving the peel intact.
4. Trim the ends from the cucumber and carrots, then cut into 4-inch pieces.
5. Cut the tomato into quarters.
6. Slice off a 1-inch piece of the ginger root.
7. Place a pitcher under the juicer's spout to collect the juice.
8. Feed each ingredient through the juicer's intake tube in the order listed.
9. When the juice stops flowing, remove the pitcher and stir the juice.
10. Serve immediately.

PER SERVING

Calories: 133| Fat: 1g | Protein: 6g | Carbohydrates: 42g | Sugar: 21g

Coconut Juice with Kale and Raspberry

Prep time: 15 minutes | Cook time: 0 minutes | Serves 1

½ cup raspberries
4 kale leaves
½ red apple
1 cup coconut water
1 tablespoon raw cacao powder

1. Wash the raspberries, kale, and apple.
2. Remove the apple core and discard. Cut the apple into quarters, leaving the peel intact.
3. Place a pitcher under the juicer's spout to collect the juice.
4. Feed the raspberries, kale, and apple through the juicer's intake tube in the order listed.
5. When the juice stops flowing, remove the pitcher, add the coconut water and raw cacao powder, and stir the juice.
6. Serve immediately.

PER SERVING

Calories: 104| Fat: 2g | Protein: 6g | Carbohydrates: 27g | Sugar: 14g

Mixed Greens with Juicy Cucumber

Prep time: 15 minutes | Cook time: 0 minutes | Serves 1

2 cups mixed greens
1 orange
1 cucumber
½ lime
1 teaspoon maca powder

1. Wash the mixed greens, orange, cucumber, and lime.
2. Peel the orange and lime, then cut into quarters.
3. Trim the ends from the cucumber, then cut into 4-inch pieces.
4. Place a pitcher under the juicer's spout to collect the juice.
5. Feed the first four ingredients through the juicer's intake tube in the order listed.
6. When the juice stops flowing, remove the pitcher, add the maca powder, and stir the juice.
7. Serve immediately.

PER SERVING

Calories: 72| Fat: 0g | Protein: 3g | Carbohydrates: 22g | Sugar: 13g

Papaya with Gingered Juice

Prep time: 10 minutes | Cook time: 0 minutes | Serves 2

1 medium kiwi, peeled
1 medium ripe papaya, peeled, seeded, cut
1 small pineapple, peeled, cored, and sliced
1 (1-inch) piece fresh ginger, peeled
½ cup fresh young coconut water

1. Peel and slice the papaya, pineapple, kiwi, and ginger. Process through a juicer.
2. Stir in the coconut water.
3. Pour the juice into glasses and enjoy.

PER SERVING

Calories: 38| Fat: 0g | Protein: 1g | Carbohydrates: 8g | Sugar: 6g

Limey Carrot Skinny Juice

Prep time: 5 minutes | Cook time: 0 minutes | Serves 1

1 cucumber
3 carrots
½ or 1 lime

1. Thoroughly wash the carrots, cucumber, and lime.
2. Run all ingredients through a juicer.
3. Pour the juice into a glass over ice and enjoy.

PER SERVING

Calories: 105| Fat: 0g | Protein: 3g | Carbohydrates: 24g | Sugar: 12g

Plumy Cucumber Juice with Lemon
Prep time: 5 minutes | Cook time: 0 minutes | Serves 1

3 plums
½ apple
1 cucumber
¼ lemon

1. Wash the plums, apple, cucumber, and lemon. Add to a juicer and process.
2. Pour into a glass and enjoy immediately.

PER SERVING

Calories: 197| Fat: 1g | Protein: 2g | Carbohydrates: 50g | Sugar: 47g

Beet with Apple Fitness Recipe
Prep time: 10 minutes | Cook time: 0 minutes | Serves 2

½ cucumber
5 carrots, halved
1 apple, quartered
½ beet
1 rib celery

1. Add the carrots, apple, cucumber, beet, and celery to a juicer and run until all ingredients are gone.
2. Pour the juice into a tall glass and enjoy immediately.

PER SERVING

Calories: 232| Fat: 1g | Protein: 4g | Carbohydrates: 57g | Sugar: 35g

Cucumber with Carrot and Berry Mix
Prep time: 10 minutes | Cook time: 0 minutes | Serves 2

1 large cucumber, peeled, cut into chunks
6 fresh strawberries, hulled
2 medium carrots, peeled
1 large red apple, quartered

1. Wash the fruits and vegetables. Peel the cucumber and carrots.
2. Pass through a juicer along with strawberries and serve over ice cubes.

PER SERVING

Calories: 130| Fat: 0g | Protein: 2g | Carbohydrates: 20g | Sugar: 30g

Gingered Pumpkin Pie Juice
Prep time: 10 minutes | Cook time: 0 minutes | Serves 1

3 carrots
1 small pumpkin, cut into cubes
1 apple (or pear)
½-inch ginger
¼ teaspoon of spices such as cinnamon, cloves or nutmeg

1. Using a sharp knife peel the pumpkin, cut into cubes. Core the apple and run through a juicer along with carrots, ginger, and pumpkin.
2. Pour into a glass, stir in the spices and drink immediately.

PER SERVING

Calories: 85| Fat: 0g | Protein: 1g | Carbohydrates: 21g | Sugar: 14g

Fresh Lemon and Carrot Juice
Prep time: 10 minutes | Cook time: 0 minutes | Serves 1

2 carrots
½-inch of fresh ginger
½ lemon
2 apples
2 ice cubes

1. Wash the lemon, carrots and apples and place in a juicer. Add the ginger and process.
2. Pour the juice in a tall glass over ice cubes and drink.

PER SERVING

Calories: 132| Fat: 0g | Protein: 1g | Carbohydrates: 32g | Sugar: 22g

Clementine Super Juice
Prep time: 10 minutes | Cook time: 0 minutes | Serves 2

1 romaine heart
5 large carrots
½ lemon, peeled
2 clementine, peeled
1-inch knob of fresh ginger

1. Peel the lemon, clementine, and carrots and run through a juicer along with romaine heart, and ginger.
2. For better results, drink this juice once a day.

PER SERVING

Calories: 76| Fat: 0g | Protein: 1g | Carbohydrates: 18g | Sugar: 9g

Beetroot with Ginger and Pear Mix

Prep time: 10 minutes | Cook time: 0 minutes | Serves 1

1 golden beetroot
3 large carrots
4 stalks celery
½ cucumber
½ thumb of ginger
1 medium pear

1. Thoroughly wash all ingredients and cut into pieces.
2. Process them through a juicer.
3. Pour the juice into a glass and enjoy.

PER SERVING

Calories: 56| Fat: 0g | Protein: 1g | Carbohydrates: 12g | Sugar: 6g

Apple Berry Skinny Juice

Prep time: 10 minutes | Cook time: 0 minutes | Serves 2

1 cup fresh blueberries
1 large cucumber, peeled and cut into chunks
¼ medium red cabbage, sliced
1 large apple, cut into eighths
Ice cubes (optional)

1. Run the blueberries, cucumber, apple, and cabbage through a juicer.
2. Pour the extracted juice into 2 glasses and enjoy.

PER SERVING

Calories: 220| Fat: 1g | Protein: 3g | Carbohydrates: 54g | Sugar: 44g

Minty Fat Burning Juice

Prep time: 10 minutes | Cook time: 0 minutes | Serves 1

1 pink grapefruit, peeled
2 oranges, peeled
1 bunch mint
1 head romaine lettuce

1. Peel the oranges and grapefruit.
2. Pass the citruses through a juicer along with mint and lettuce and enjoy.

PER SERVING

Calories: 185| Fat: 4g | Protein: 5g | Carbohydrates: 27g | Sugar: 37g

Simple Broccoli Weight Loss Juice

Prep time: 5 minutes | Cook time: 0 minutes | Serves 1

2 large Broccoli raw
2 Celery stalks raw
1 Apple, raw
1 Lemon, raw

1. Place the whole broccoli in the juicer and juice it. The white pith should be left on the lemon.
2. Put in the other ingredients and juice until smooth. Serve in a tall glass.
3. Enjoy!

PER SERVING

Calories: 132 | Fat: 1g | Protein: 3g | Carbohydrates: 34g | Sugar: 22mg

Almond Slim Me Juice

Prep time: 6 minutes | Cook time: 0 minutes | Serves 2

1 apple
4-5 raspberries
1 kiwifruit
1 banana
4 almonds

1. Remove stem from apple. Peel banana.
2. Run all ingredients through a juicer
3. Serve fresh

PER SERVING

Calories: 125 | Fat: 2g | Protein: 2g | Carbohydrates: 29g | Sugar: 18mg

Peachy Power Green Tea

Prep time: 6 minutes | Cook time: 0 minutes | Serves 2

½ peeled banana
½ cup mango chunks
1 cup peach juice
1 tablespoon ground flax seeds
1 tablespoon green tea powder

1. Process all ingredients in a juicer.
2. Serve fresh

PER SERVING

Calories: 206 | Fat: 1.4g | Protein: 2g | Carbohydrates: 28g | Sugar: 22mg

Orange Grapefruit Slim Juice

Prep time: 5 minutes | Cook time: 0 minutes | Serves 1

3 oranges
1 grapefruit

1. Peel the oranges and grapefruit.
2. Run through a juicer
3. Serve fresh

PER SERVING

Calories: 404 | Fat: 2g | Protein: 8g | Carbohydrates: 100g | Sugar: 17mg

Blackberry Grape Goodness

Prep time: 5 minutes | Cook time: 0 minutes | Serves 2

1 cup blackberries
2 cups red grapes
2 asparagus

1. Run all ingredients through a juicer
2. Serve fresh

PER SERVING

Calories: 223 | Fat: 0.4g | Protein: 3g | Carbohydrates: 57g | Sugar: 49mg

Cabbage Berry Power Blast

Prep time: 10 minutes | Cook time: 0 minutes | Serves 1

2 small green zucchinis
½ cup of small green cabbage
2 small green apples
4 green kale leaves
1 cup of blueberries
1 mango
½ medium cucumber

1. Wash all produce. Trim the zucchini ends. Dice the cabbage to fit into the juicer. Quarter apples and discard seeds.
2. Remove any stems from the blueberries.
3. Peel mango and discard seed. Place all produce into your juicer. If you would like to make your green juice a little sweeter, add ⅓ cup of shredded coconut to the juice.
4. This can be blended with or served over ice if desired. Stir and drink immediately.

PER SERVING

Calories: 674 | Fat: 5g | Protein: 10g | Carbohydrates: 165g | Sugar: 140mg3

Sunny Veggie Delight

Prep time: 10 minutes | Cook time: 0 minutes | Serves 2

2 large broccoli stalks
¼ head of green cabbage
2 celery stalks
¼ head of romaine lettuce
2 green apples
1 orange
2 carrots

1. Wash all produce. Chop broccoli, romaine, and cabbage to fit into your juicer. Quarter apples and remove all seeds.
2. Peel orange and carrots. Remove all seeds from the orange.
3. Place all produce into your juicer. This can be served over ice if desired. Stir and drink immediately.

PER SERVING

Calories: 240 | Fat: 1.4g | Protein: 7.5g | Carbohydrates: 58g | Sugar: 27mg

Green Slimmer Juice

Prep time: 10 minutes | Cook time: 0 minutes | Serves 2

½ bunch of spinach
1 cup of green cabbage
2 celery stalks
½ of a beet
2 green apples
1 cucumber
1 orange

1. Wash all produce. Roll spinach leaves to fit into your juicer. Shred cabbage. Quarter green apples and remove all seeds.
2. Peel orange and remove all seeds. Place all ingredients into your juicer. This can be served over ice if desired.
3. Stir and drink immediately.

PER SERVING

Calories: 202 | Fat: 1g | Protein: 6g | Carbohydrates: 48g | Sugar: 24mg

Slim Garden Delight

Prep time: 10 minutes | Cook time: 0 minutes | Serves 1

5 medium carrots
1 medium apple
1 cucumber
1 thumb ginger root
1 medium pear
2 handful spinach
½ of fruit lemon (Recommended peeled for less-bitter taste)

1. Wash the fruits and vegetables thoroughly
2. Put them through juicer and enjoy

PER SERVING

Calories: 368 | Fat: 2g | Protein: 7g | Carbohydrates: 91g | Sugar: 55mg

Chapter 8
Detoxifying and Cleansing Juices

Garlicky Radish Detox Juice
Prep time: 5 minutes | Cook time: 0 minutes | Serves 1

2 garlic cloves
3 medium carrots
1 medium beet
1 radish
A handful of parsley

1. Peel the beet, carrots, radish, and garlic and wash the parsley.
2. Run all ingredients through a juicer and drink immediately.
3. Great to drink 1-2 times a day.

PER SERVING

Calories: 90| Fat: 0g | Protein: 2g | Carbohydrates: 21g | Sugar: 11g

Cabbage and Cucumber Body Cleanse
Prep time: 5 minutes | Cook time: 0 minutes | Serves 1

½ medium cucumber
1 smallish beet
2 red or green cabbage leaves
4 medium carrots

1. Thoroughly wash the vegetables.
2. Cut the carrot ends and discard the greens.
3. Peel the beet and quarter it.
4. Pass all the ingredients through a juicer, pour into a glass and drink immediately.

PER SERVING

Calories: 56| Fat: 0g | Protein: 1g | Carbohydrates: 13g | Sugar: 6g

Cucumber and Cabbage Daily Detox Juice
Prep time: 10 minutes | Cook time: 0 minutes | Serves 1

1 cup Napa cabbage
1 large cucumber
1 cup green or red cabbage
1 Granny Smith apple
4 stalks celery
1 cup greens (kale, chard, spinach etc.)
4 carrots
2 bell peppers (any color)
3 red or golden beets (or a combination)
1 lemon
1 lime
1 to 2-inch piece of ginger root

1. Thoroughly wash all the vegetables and cut into chunks.
2. Process through a juicer and drink.

PER SERVING

Calories: 227| Fat: 1g | Protein: 7g | Carbohydrates: 52g | Sugar: 27g

Gingered Veggie Detox Mix
Prep time: 10 minutes | Cook time: 0 minutes | Serves 1

2 medium beets
3 medium tomatoes
3 long carrots, cut
Small piece of ginger

1. Wash all the vegetables and pass through a juicer.
2. Pour the juice into a glass and enjoy.

PER SERVING

Calories: 71| Fat: 0g | Protein: 2g | Carbohydrates: 16g | Sugar: 9g

Gingered Cleansing Juice
Prep time: 5 minutes | Cook time: 0 minutes | Serves 2

2 pounds (900 g) carrots, peeled
¼ cup fresh lime juice
Small piece ginger

1. Wash the carrots and run through a juicer along with a small piece of ginger.
2. Add the lime juice, stir well and drink.

PER SERVING

Calories: 166| Fat: 0g | Protein: 4g | Carbohydrates: 40g | Sugar: 16g

Lemony Super Cleanse
Prep time: 5 minutes | Cook time: 0 minutes | Serves 1

1 bunch celery
½ head purple cabbage
1 lemon

1. Process the celery, purple cabbage, and lemon through a juicer.
2. Pour into a glass over ice and enjoy.

PER SERVING

Calories: 51| Fat: 0g | Protein: 2g | Carbohydrates: 12g | Sugar: 6g

Basil with Spinach Cleansing Juice
Prep time: 5 minutes | Cook time: 0 minutes | Serves 1

5 tomatoes
1 cup of basil
2 handfuls of spinach
½ cucumber, unpeeled

1. Wash all the produce under running water.
2. Run the spinach and basil through a juicer followed by tomatoes and cucumber.
3. Pour the juice into a tall glass and enjoy.

Lemon and Ginger Detox Juice

Prep time: 10 minutes | Cook time: 0 minutes | Serves 1

½ medium cucumber
2 medium stalks celery
4 romaine heart leaves or 2 outer leaves
2 kale leaves
1 cup spinach
1 medium green apple
1 lemon, rind and pith removed
1 slice ginger

1. Thoroughly wash all ingredients and pass through a juicer.
2. Pour the juice into a glass and enjoy.

PER SERVING

Calories: 154| Fat: 1g | Protein: 3g | Carbohydrates: 37g | Sugar: 25g

Zucchini and Celery Skin Detox Juice

Prep time: 15 minutes | Cook time: 0 minutes | Serves 1

1 cup spinach
1 cup cubed sweet potato
3 celery ribs
1 zucchini
1 cucumber
½ lemon

1. Wash all the ingredients.
2. Peel the sweet potato and cut into small cubes.
3. Trim the ends from the celery, zucchini, and cucumber, then cut into 4-inch pieces.
4. Peel the lemon half and cut into quarters.
5. Place a pitcher under the juicer's spout to collect the juice.
6. Feed each ingredient through the juicer's intake tube in the order listed.
7. When the juice stops flowing, remove the pitcher and stir the juice.
8. Serve immediately.

PER SERVING

Calories: 57| Fat: 2g | Protein: 0g | Carbohydrates: 5g | Sugar: 15g

Turmeric with Ginger Green Juice

Prep time: 5 minutes | Cook time: 0 minutes | Serves 1

6 carrots
1 romaine heart
2 celery ribs
1 orange
Fresh ginger root
Fresh turmeric root

1. Wash all the ingredients.
2. Trim the ends from the carrots and celery, then cut into 4-inch pieces.
3. Peel the orange and cut into quarters.
4. Slice off ½-inch pieces of the ginger root and the turmeric root.
5. Place a pitcher under the juicer's spout to collect the juice.
6. Feed each ingredient through the juicer's intake tube in the order listed.
7. When the juice stops flowing, remove the pitcher and stir the juice.
8. Serve immediately.

PER SERVING

Calories: 151| Fat: 2g | Protein: 7g | Carbohydrates: 46g | Sugar: 24g

Artichoke with Apple Beauty Juice

Prep time: 20 minutes | Cook time: 0 minutes | Serves 1

1 artichoke
1 green apple
1 cup spinach
1 celery rib

1. Wash all the ingredients.
2. Prepare the artichoke per the instructions in the Preparation Tip.
3. Remove the apple core and discard. Cut the apple into quarters, leaving the peel intact.
4. Trim the ends from the celery, then cut into 4-inch pieces.
5. Place a pitcher under the juicer's spout to collect the juice. Then, feed each ingredient through the juicer's intake tube in the order listed.
6. When the juice stops flowing, remove the pitcher and stir the juice.
7. Serve immediately.

PER SERVING

Calories: 75| Fat: 0g | Protein: 4g | Carbohydrates: 25g | Sugar: 12g

Kiwi with Limey Spinach Mix

Prep time: 15 minutes | Cook time: 0 minutes | Serves 2

4 kiwis
4 cups spinach
1 cucumber
1 lime
Pinch sea salt

1. Wash the kiwis, spinach, cucumber, and lime.
2. Trim the ends from the cucumber, then cut into 4-inch pieces.
3. Peel the kiwis and lime and cut them into quarters.
4. Place a pitcher under the juicer's spout to collect the juice.
5. Feed the first four ingredients through the juicer's intake tube in the order listed.
6. When the juice stops flowing, remove the pitcher, add the sea salt, and stir the juice.
7. Serve immediately.

PER SERVING

Calories: 145| Fat: 2g | Protein: 6g | Carbohydrates: 43g | Sugar: 22g

Broccoli with Mustardy Turmeric Juice

Prep time: 15 minutes | Cook time: 0 minutes | Serves 1

8 carrots
4 mustard green leaves
3 lemons
2 cups broccoli
Fresh turmeric root

1. Wash all the ingredients.
2. Trim the ends from the carrots, then cut into 4-inch pieces.
3. Peel the lemons and cut into quarters.
4. Remove the stalk from the broccoli crown with a knife and discard or save to juice later. Cut the crown into small florets.
5. Slice off a 2-inch piece of the turmeric root.
6. Place a pitcher under the juicer's spout to collect the juice.
7. Feed each ingredient through the juicer's intake tube in the order listed.
8. When the juice stops flowing, remove the pitcher and stir the juice.
9. Serve immediately.

PER SERVING

Calories: 171| Fat: 2g | Protein: 9g | Carbohydrates: 55g | Sugar: 22g

Fennel with Kale Antioxidant Juice

Prep time: 15 minutes | Cook time: 0 minutes | Serves 1

4 kale leaves
½ cup blackberries
½ green apple
1 cup broccoli
1 cucumber
½ fennel bulb

1. Wash all the ingredients.
2. Remove the apple core and discard. Cut the apple into quarters, leaving the peel intact.
3. Remove the stalk from the broccoli crown with a knife and discard or save to juice later. Cut the crown into small florets.
4. Trim the ends from the cucumber, then cut into 4-inch pieces.
5. Remove the stalks and fronds from the fennel and save for later. Cut the bulb into quarters.
6. Place a pitcher under the juicer's spout to collect the juice.
7. Feed each ingredient through the juicer's intake tube in the order listed.
8. When the juice stops flowing, remove the pitcher and stir the juice.
9. Serve immediately.

PER SERVING

Calories: 138| Fat: 2g | Protein: 10g | Carbohydrates: 41g | Sugar: 18g

Arugula Detox Juice with Celery

Prep time: 5 minutes | Cook time: 0 minutes | Serves 1

Handful arugula
1-inch piece fresh ginger root
1 large celery stalk
1 medium green apple

1. Peel, cut, deseed, and/or chop the ingredients as needed.
2. Place a container under the juicer's spout.
3. Feed the ingredients in the order listed, through the juicer.
4. Alternate ingredients, finishing with the apple or the celery.
5. Stir the juice and pour into glasses to serve.

PER SERVING

Calories: 138| Fat: 2g | Protein: 10g | Carbohydrates: 41g | Sugar: 18g

Parsley with Cabbage Detox

Prep time: 10 minutes | Cook time: 0 minutes | Serves 2

1 cup red cabbage
2 cups black, purple, or red grapes
12 parsley sprigs
2 large celery stalks

1. Peel, cut, deseed, and/or chop the ingredients as needed.
2. Place a container under the juicer's spout.
3. Feed the ingredients in the order listed, through the juicer.
4. Alternate ingredients, finishing with the apple or the celery.
5. Stir the juice and pour into glasses to serve.

PER SERVING

Calories: 133| Fat: 0g | Protein: 2g | Carbohydrates: 32g | Sugar: 25g

Simple Romaine Detox

Prep time: 5 minutes | Cook time: 0 minutes | Serves 2

1 cup red cabbage
1 firm pear
8 medium romaine leaves

1. Peel, cut, deseed, and/or chop the ingredients as needed.
2. Place a container under the juicer's spout.
3. Feed the ingredients in the order listed, through the juicer.
4. Alternate ingredients, finishing with the romaine.
5. Stir the juice and pour into glasses to serve.

PER SERVING

Calories: 33| Fat: 0g | Protein: 2g | Carbohydrates: 7g | Sugar: 3g

Cilantro with Pear Detox Delight

Prep time: 5 minutes | Cook time: 0 minutes | Serves 1

1 medium zucchini
1 firm pear
Handful cilantro
½ large cucumber

1. Peel, cut, deseed, and/or chop the ingredients as needed.
2. Place a container under the juicer's spout.
3. Feed the ingredients in the order listed, through the juicer.
4. Alternate ingredients, finishing with the cucumber.
5. Stir the juice and pour into glasses to serve.

PER SERVING

Calories: 51| Fat: 0g | Protein: 1g | Carbohydrates: 15g | Sugar: 10g

Plum with Kale Cocktail

Prep time: 10 minutes | Cook time: 0 minutes | Serves 2

1 cup red cabbage
2 medium kale leaves
1 medium red apple
½ red or black plum
½ large cucumber

1. Peel, cut, deseed, and/or chop the ingredients as needed.
2. Place a container under the juicer's spout.
3. Feed the ingredients in the order listed, through the juicer.
4. Alternate ingredients, finishing with the cucumber.
5. Stir the juice and pour into glasses to serve.

PER SERVING

Calories: 80| Fat: 0g | Protein: 1g | Carbohydrates: 20g | Sugar: 15g

Zucchini with Bok Choy Blend

Prep time: 10 minutes | Cook time: 0 minutes | Serves 2

1 medium zucchini
2 cups black, purple, or red grapes
4 small Bok choy stems

1. Peel, cut, deseed, and/or chop the ingredients as needed.
2. Place a container under the juicer's spout.
3. Feed the ingredients in the order listed, through the juicer.
4. Alternate ingredients, finishing with the Bok choy.
5. Stir the juice and pour into glasses to serve.

PER SERVING

Calories: 105| Fat: 0g | Protein: 1g | Carbohydrates: 23g | Sugar: 23g

Parsley and Pear with Cleansing Carrot

Prep time: 5 minutes | Cook time: 0 minutes | Serves 2

4 large carrots
Handful parsley
1 firm pear

1. Peel, cut, deseed, and/or chop the ingredients as needed.
2. Place a container under the juicer's spout.
3. Feed the ingredients in the order listed, through the juicer.
4. Alternate ingredients, finishing with the pear.
5. Stir the juice and pour into glasses to serve.

PER SERVING

Calories: 51| Fat: 0g | Protein: 1g | Carbohydrates: 14g | Sugar: 7g

Cilantro with Zucchini Fresh Detox
Prep time: 10 minutes | Cook time: 0 minutes | Serves 2

4 large dandelion leaves
2 medium radishes
1 medium zucchini
Handful cilantro
1 cup black, purple, or red grapes
1 small orange, red, or yellow bell pepper

1. Peel, cut, deseed, and/or chop the ingredients as needed.
2. Place a container under the juicer's spout.
3. Feed the ingredients in the order listed, through the juicer.
4. Alternate ingredients, finishing with the bell pepper.
5. Stir the juice and pour into glasses to serve.

PER SERVING

Calories: 33| Fat: 1g | Protein: 10g | Carbohydrates: 21g | Sugar: 2g

Cucumber with Carrot-Apple Detox
Prep time: 10 minutes | Cook time: 0 minutes | Serves 2

4 medium carrots
12 parsley sprigs
1 medium apple
2 medium celery stalks
1 large cucumber

1. Peel, cut, deseed, and/or chop the ingredients as needed.
2. Place a container under the juicer's spout.
3. Feed the ingredients in the order listed, through the juicer.
4. Alternate ingredients, finishing with the cucumber.
5. Stir the juice and pour into glasses to serve.

PER SERVING

Calories: 119| Fat: 1g | Protein: 2g | Carbohydrates: 28g | Sugar: 17g

Turmeric with Cleansing Carrot Juice
Prep time: 10 minutes | Cook time: 0 minutes | Serves 2

4 medium carrots
1-inch piece fresh turmeric root
Handful parsley
1 large orange, red, or yellow bell pepper
Freshly ground black pepper (optional)

1. Peel, cut, deseed, and/or chop the ingredients as needed.
2. Place a container under the juicer's spout.
3. Feed the ingredients in the order listed, through the juicer.
4. Alternate the produce, finishing with the bell pepper.
5. Stir the black pepper (if using) directly into the juice to increase your absorption of the curcumin in the turmeric.

PER SERVING

Calories: 50| Fat: 0g | Protein: 1g | Carbohydrates: 11g | Sugar: 6g

Cilantro with Spiced Spinach Detox Mix
Prep time: 10 minutes | Cook time: 0 minutes | Serves 2

1 large orange, red, or yellow bell pepper
2 large carrots
Handful spinach
1 small lemon
1-inch piece fresh turmeric root
Handful cilantro
½ large cucumber
Freshly ground black pepper (optional)

1. Peel, cut, deseed, and/or chop the ingredients as needed.
2. Place a container under the juicer's spout.
3. Feed the ingredients in the order listed, through the juicer.
4. Alternate the produce, finishing with the cucumber.
5. Stir the black pepper (if using) directly into the juice to increase your absorption of the curcumin in the turmeric.

PER SERVING

Calories: 96| Fat: 2g | Protein: 2g | Carbohydrates: 22g | Sugar: 10g

Parsley with Cauliflower Cleanse
Prep time: 10 minutes | Cook time: 0 minutes | Serves 2

1 cup cauliflower
1 firm pear
8 parsley sprigs
4 large celery stalks

1. Peel, cut, deseed, and/or chop the ingredients as needed.
2. Place a container under the juicer's spout.
3. Feed the ingredients in the order listed, through the juicer.
4. Alternate ingredients, finishing with the celery.
5. Stir the juice and pour into glasses to serve.

PER SERVING

Calories: 20| Fat: 0g | Protein: 1g | Carbohydrates: 4g | Sugar: 2g

Pear Berry Cleanser
Prep time: 10 minutes | Cook time: 0 minutes | Serves 2

1 cup mixed berries
1 firm pear
4 cups spinach
4 medium celery stalks

1. Peel, cut, deseed, and/or chop the ingredients as needed.
2. Place a container under the juicer's spout.
3. Feed the ingredients in the order listed, through the juicer.
4. Juice the berries and the pear first, then alternate the remaining ingredients, finishing with the celery.
5. Stir the juice and pour into glasses to serve.

PER SERVING

Calories: 294| Fat: 6g | Protein: 5g | Carbohydrates: 56g | Sugar: 31g

Kale Pineapple Cleansing Juice

Prep time: 5 minutes | Cook time: 0 minutes | Serves 2

4 kale leaves
2 cups pineapple

1. Peel, cut, deseed, and/or chop the ingredients as needed.
2. Place a container under the juicer's spout.
3. Feed the ingredients in the order listed, through the juicer.
4. Alternate ingredients, finishing with the pineapple.
5. Stir the juice and pour into glasses to serve.

PER SERVING

Calories: 150| Fat: 0g | Protein: 1g | Carbohydrates: 39g | Sugar: 36g

Collard Veggie Cleansing Juice

Prep time: 15 minutes | Cook time: 0 minutes | Serves 2

1 red bell pepper
2 large carrots
1 small collard leaf
1 medium kale leaf
½ large cucumber
Handful cilantro or parsley
1 medium red apple

1. Peel, cut, deseed, and/or chop the ingredients as needed.
2. Place a container under the juicer's spout.
3. Feed the ingredients in the order listed, through the juicer.
4. Alternate ingredients, finishing with the apple.
5. Stir the juice and pour into glasses to serve.

PER SERVING

Calories: 94| Fat: 0g | Protein: 2g | Carbohydrates: 23g | Sugar: 15g

Spinach with Purple Pineapple

Prep time: 10 minutes | Cook time: 0 minutes | Serves 2

1 cup red cabbage
Handful spinach
1 cup pineapple
2 Cara or other small oranges, peeled

1. Peel, cut, deseed, and/or chop the ingredients as needed.
2. Place a container under the juicer's spout.
3. Feed the ingredients in the order listed, through the juicer.
4. Alternate ingredients, finishing with the orange or the pineapple.
5. Stir the juice and pour into glasses to serve.

PER SERVING

Calories: 88| Fat: 01g | Protein: 23g | Carbohydrates: 20g | Sugar: 20g

Radish with Zucchini Coconut Cleanse

Prep time: 15 minutes | Cook time: 0 minutes | Serves 3

4-inch piece broccoli stem
4 large kale leaves
2 medium radishes
1 medium zucchini
1 firm pear
1 medium apple
1 cup fresh coconut water

1. Peel, cut, deseed, and/or chop the ingredients as needed.
2. Place a container under the juicer's spout.
3. Feed the ingredients in the order listed, through the juicer.
4. Alternate the produce, finishing with the apple.
5. Stir the coconut water directly into the juice.

PER SERVING

Calories: 72| Fat: 0g | Protein: 1g | Carbohydrates: 17g | Sugar: 13g

Broccoli with Apple Cleansing Juice

Prep time: 10 minutes | Cook time: 0 minutes | Serves 2

4-inch piece broccoli stem
4 large Swiss chard leaves
1 medium apple
2 large celery stalks

1. Peel, cut, deseed, and/or chop the ingredients as needed.
2. Place a container under the juicer's spout.
3. Feed the ingredients in the order listed, through the juicer.
4. Alternate the produce, finishing with the celery or the apple.
5. Stir the juice and pour into glasses to serve.

PER SERVING

Calories: 51| Fat: 0g | Protein: 0g | Carbohydrates: 13g | Sugar: 10g

Grapy Cabbage Cleansing Juice

Prep time: 10 minutes | Cook time: 0 minutes | Serves 2

1 cup red cabbage
2 cups black, purple, or red grapes
12 parsley sprigs
1 medium apple

1. Peel, cut, deseed, and/or chop the ingredients as needed.
2. Place a container under the juicer's spout.
3. Feed the ingredients in the order listed, through the juicer.
4. Alternate the produce, finishing with the apple.
5. Stir the juice and pour into glasses to serve

PER SERVING

Calories: 167| Fat: 0g | Protein: 2g | Carbohydrates: 44g | Sugar: 35g

Watermelon with Pineapple Cleansing Mix

Prep time: 10 minutes | Cook time: 0 minutes | Serves 2

2 large kale leaves
1 cup pineapple
2 cups watermelon

1. Peel, cut, deseed, and/or chop the ingredients as needed.
2. Place a container under the juicer's spout.
3. Feed the ingredients in the order listed, through the juicer.
4. Alternate ingredients, finishing with the watermelon or the pineapple.
5. Stir the juice and pour into glasses to serve

PER SERVING

Calories: 121| Fat: 0g | Protein: 1g | Carbohydrates: 31g | Sugar: 28g

Kale Apple Cleansing Juice

Prep time: 10 minutes | Cook time: 0 minutes | Serves 2

2 large carrots
2 large kale leaves
½ red apple
1 cup watermelon

1. Peel, cut, deseed, and/or chop the ingredients as needed.
2. Place a container under the juicer's spout.
3. Feed the ingredients in the order listed, through the juicer.
4. Alternate ingredients, finishing with the watermelon.
1. Stir the juice and pour into glasses to serve

PER SERVING

Calories: 84| Fat: 0g | Protein: 1g | Carbohydrates: 20g | Sugar: 14g

Bok Choy with Kiwi Refresher

Prep time: 10 minutes | Cook time: 0 minutes | Serves 2

2 large Bok choy stems
2 kiwifruits
1 cup watermelon

1. Peel, cut, deseed, and/or chop the ingredients as needed.
2. Place a container under the juicer's spout.
3. Feed the ingredients in the order listed, through the juicer.
4. Alternate ingredients, finishing with the watermelon or the pineapple.
5. Stir the juice and pour into glasses to serve

PER SERVING

Calories: 28| Fat: 1g | Protein: 1g | Carbohydrates: 6g | Sugar: 5g

Potato Kale Detox

Prep time: 10 minutes | Cook time: 0 minutes | Serves 3

4 extra-large carrots
2 large kale leaves
1 small, sweet potato, peeled

1. Peel, cut, deseed, and/or chop the ingredients as needed.
2. Place a container under the juicer's spout.
3. Feed the ingredients in the order listed, through the juicer.
4. Alternate ingredients, finishing with the sweet potato.
5. Stir the juice and pour into glasses to serve

PER SERVING

Calories: 27| Fat: 1g | Protein: 1g | Carbohydrates: 9g | Sugar: 2g

Lemony Spinach Veggie Cleanser

Prep time: 15 minutes | Cook time: 0 minutes | Serves 2

3 cups spinach
½ small, sweet potato, peeled
8 parsley sprigs
½ medium lemon
4 large celery stalks

1. Peel, cut, deseed, and/or chop the ingredients as needed.
2. Place a container under the juicer's spout.
3. Feed the ingredients in the order listed, through the juicer.
4. Alternate ingredients, finishing with celery.
5. Stir the juice and pour into glasses to serve.

PER SERVING

Calories: 20| Fat: 0g | Protein: 2g | Carbohydrates: 4g | Sugar: 1g

Turmeric with Potato and Orange Roots

Prep time: 10 minutes | Cook time: 0 minutes | Serves 2

4 large carrots
1-inch piece fresh turmeric root
1 small, sweet potato, peeled
Freshly ground black pepper (optional)

1. Peel, cut, deseed, and/or chop the ingredients as needed.
2. Place a container under the juicer's spout.
3. Feed the ingredients in the order listed, through the juicer.
4. Alternate the produce, finishing with the sweet potato.
5. Stir the black pepper (if using) directly into the juice to increase your absorption of the curcumin in the turmeric.

PER SERVING

Calories: 86| Fat: 0g | Protein: 2g | Carbohydrates: 20g | Sugar: 9g

Red Apple with Turmeric Detox

Prep time: 5 minutes | Cook time: 0 minutes | Serves 1

1 medium golden or red beet
1-inch piece fresh ginger root
1-inch piece fresh turmeric root
12 parsley sprigs
1 medium red apple
1 large cucumber
Freshly ground black pepper (optional)

1. Peel, cut, deseed, and/or chop the ingredients as needed.
2. Place a container under the juicer's spout.
3. Feed the ingredients in the order listed, through the juicer.
4. Alternate the produce, finishing with the cucumber.
5. Stir the black pepper (if using) directly into the juice to increase your absorption of the curcumin in the turmeric.

PER SERVING

Calories: 84| Fat: 0g | Protein: 2g | Carbohydrates: 20g | Sugar: 14g

Spinach with Celery and Orange Cleanser

Prep time: 10 minutes | Cook time: 0 minutes | Serves 2
3 large carrots
2 large celery stalks
Handful spinach
8 parsley sprigs
2 medium oranges, peeled
½ large cucumber

1. Peel, cut, deseed, and/or chop the ingredients as needed.
2. Place a container under the juicer's spout.
3. Feed the ingredients in the order listed, through the juicer.
4. Alternate ingredients, finishing with the cucumber.
5. Stir the juice and pour into glasses to serve.

PER SERVING

Calories: 57| Fat: 0g | Protein: 2g | Carbohydrates: 13g | Sugar: 6g

Lemony Liver Detox Juice

Prep time: 10 minutes | Cook time: 0 minutes | Serves 2
1 small baby Bok choy
3 large kale leaves
1 medium apple
1 small lemon
½-inch piece gingerroot

1. Peel, cut, deseed, and/or chop the ingredients as needed.
2. Place a container under the juicer's spout.
3. Feed the ingredients one at a time, in the order listed, through the juicer.
4. Stir the juice and pour into glasses to serve.

PER SERVING

Calories: 53| Fat: 0g | Protein: 0g | Carbohydrates: 14g | Sugar: 10g

Beet and Apple Red Detox

Prep time: 10 minutes | Cook time: 0 minutes | Serves 2

½ medium red beet
2 beet stems with greens, or handful spinach
4 parsley sprigs
3 large carrots
1 small lemon
1 medium red apple

1. Peel, cut, deseed, and/or chop the ingredients as needed.
2. Place a container under the juicer's spout.
3. Feed the ingredients in the order listed, through the juicer.
4. Alternate ingredients, finishing with apple.
5. Stir the juice and pour into glasses to serve.

PER SERVING

Calories: 1,202| Fat: 107g | Protein: 17g | Carbohydrates: 50g | Sugar: 12g

Kale with Chard and Celery Cleanse

Prep time: 15 minutes | Cook time: 0 minutes | Serves 2

2 large celery stalks
1 large kale leaf
2 cups spinach
1 large Swiss chard leaf
2 green apples
8 parsley or cilantro sprigs
1 large cucumber

1. Peel, cut, deseed, and/or chop the ingredients as needed.
2. Place a container under the juicer's spout.
3. Feed the ingredients in the order listed, through the juicer.
4. Alternate ingredients, finishing with the cucumber.
5. Stir the juice and pour into glasses to serve.

PER SERVING

Calories: 127| Fat: 0g | Protein: 3g | Carbohydrates: 31g | Sugar: 21g

Coconut Limeade with Cilantro Juice

Prep time: 10 minutes | Cook time: 0 minutes | Serves 2
¼ medium lemon
¼ medium lime, peeled
1-inch piece fresh ginger root
Handful cilantro
1-pound carrots
½ cup fresh coconut water

1. Peel, cut, deseed, and/or chop the ingredients as needed.
2. Place a container under the juicer's spout.
3. Feed the ingredients in the order listed, through the juicer.
4. Alternate ingredients, finishing with celery.
5. Stir the coconut water directly into the juice.

PER SERVING

Calories: 213| Fat: 1g | Protein: 5g | Carbohydrates: 29g | Sugar: 35g

Icey Super Detox Juice

Prep time: 10 minutes | Cook time: 0 minutes | Serves 1

4 carrots
3 apples
2 celery stalks
1 cup of spinach
1 chunk of ginger

1. Put all ingredients through the juicer.
2. Add Ice.
3. Enjoy

PER SERVING

Calories: 398 | Fat: 2g | Protein: 5g | Carbohydrates: 101g | Sugar: 69g

Red Carroty Cleansing Juice

Prep time: 10 minutes | Cook time: 0 minutes | Serves 1

1 full beet root, cut into slices
1 inch piece of ginger
2 large carrots
1 large apple
2 thick slices peeled, and de-seeded cucumbers

1. To complete this recipe, use your juice to carefully process the slices of beets.
2. Follow the beets with ginger, the carrots, apple, and finally the cucumber slices.
3. This drink will help detox your body by providing plenty of fiber that is particularly abundant in the beets.
4. The ginger helps act as a natural healer and can help one feel calm and collected which is essential in any journey to well-being, detoxification, and weight loss.

PER SERVING

Calories: 265 | Fat: 4g | Protein: 8g | Carbohydrates: 54g | Sugar: 36g

Lemony Red Velvet

Prep time: 10 minutes | Cook time: 0 minutes | Serves 1

2 medium apples
4 medium carrots
¼ head small red cabbage
½ thumb ginger root ginger root
4 handful spinach
½ of fruit lemon (Recommended peeled for less-bitter taste)

1. Wash the fruits and vegetables thoroughly
2. Put them through juicer and enjoy

PER SERVING

Calories: 208 | Fat: 1.4g | Protein: 6g | Carbohydrates: 66g | Sugar: 56mg

Melony Tomato Cleanse

Prep time: 10 minutes | Cook time: 0 minutes | Serves 1

1 large tomato
1 large wedge watermelon
Lemon – ½ of fruit (Recommended peeled for less-bitter taste)

1. Wash the fruits and vegetables thoroughly
2. Put them through juicer and enjoy

PER SERVING

Calories: 135 | Fat: 1g | Protein: 4g | Carbohydrates: 37g | Sugar: 6mg

Jalapeno Ginger Gold with Lime

Prep time: 10 minutes | Cook time: 0 minutes | Serves 2

2 Lemons with Skin and only if organic
1 Lime with skin and only if organic
10 Ribs of Celery (organic if possible)
2 inch of Fresh Ginger (organic if possible)
2 cups of Parsley (organic if possible)
2 Apples (any kind and organic if possible)
½ Jalapeno (this is a hot ingredient so be careful)

ALTERNATIVE TO THE JALAPENO:

Sprinkle some cayenne pepper on top of your tonic drink when it's finished!

1. Peel the ginger and the apples.
2. Next cut and chop the thoroughly washed veggies and fruits.
3. Put your ingredients into your favorite juicer and strictly follow the directions of the manual that comes with your machine.
4. Your juicer manual will tell you what buttons to push and what speed to use.
5. Juice the softer textures first.
6. You will see that when you are juicing the crunchier veggies and fruits they will help you push the softer and more delicate fruits and veggies through the blades.
7. If you are not using a juicer and only have a blender available, make sure to first strain the juice from the lime and lemons.
8. Once it is finished you can either leave the pulp inside or take it out. This is totally up to your preference.
9. In this case you have to add the juices back to the blender and proceed from there.
10. Juice and blend the juice with the rest of your ingredients together as per instructions.
11. You can always add some raw honey or sweetener depending on your goal with these juices. If the juice is too strong for you, you might also add some ice cubes or source water.
12. Enjoy this Vitamin C enriched delicious tonic!

PER SERVING

Calories: 400 | Fat: 26g | Protein: 13g | Carbohydrates: 31g | Sugar: 20g

Swiss-Melon Elixir

Prep time: 10 minutes | Cook time: 0 minutes | Serves 1

2 Apples (organic if possible)
½ Cantaloupe (organic if possible)
½ Honeydew (organic if possible)
6-8 leaves Kale (organic if possible)
6-8 leaves Swiss Chard (organic if possible)

1. Peel the apples and scrape out the juicy contents of the melons.
2. Next cut and chop the fruits and veggies.
3. Put all the fruits and veggies from the ingredients list into your favorite juicer or blender or a combination of juicer/blender (Nutribullet) and strictly follow the directions of the manual that comes with your machine.
4. Juice the softer textures first.
5. You will see that when you are juicing the crunchier veggies and fruits they will help you push the softer and more delicate fruits and veggies through the blades.
6. Juice and blend all the ingredients from the list above together as per instructions.
7. You can always add some raw honey or sweetener depending on your goal with these juices. If the juice is too strong for you, you might also add some ice cubes or source water.
8. Enjoy this refreshing and hydrating Elixir that will beautify and heal you from the inside out!

PER SERVING

Calories: 203 | Fat: 1g | Protein: 2g | Carbohydrates: 53g | Sugar: 39g

Whole Juicy Detox Drink

Prep time: 10 minutes | Cook time: 0 minutes | Serves 1

3 ribs of celery (organic if possible)
1 big handful of spinach (organic if possible or organic baby spinach)
2 stalks of asparagus (organic if possible)
1 large tomato (organic if possible)
1 carrot (organic if possible)

1. Peel the tomato, carrot and the asparagus.
2. Next cut and chop the veggies.
3. Put all the fruits and veggies from the ingredients list into your favorite juicer or blender or a combination of juicer/blender (Nutribullet) and strictly follow the directions of the manual that comes with your machine.
4. Your blender manual will tell you what buttons to push and what speed to use.
5. Juice the softer textures first.
6. You will see that when you are juicing the crunchier veggies they will help you push the softer and more delicate ones through the blades.
7. Juice and blend all the ingredients from the list above together as per instructions.
8. Enjoy!

PER SERVING

Calories: 54 | Fat: 0.5g | Protein: 2.5g | Carbohydrates: 12g | Sugar: 7g

Berry Coconut Veggie Detox

Prep time: 15 minutes | Cook time: 0 minutes | Serves 1

2 small zucchini (organic if possible)
2 red apples (organic if possible)
4 green kale leaves (organic if possible)
4 white or purple cauliflower florets (organic if possible)
1½ cup blueberries (organic if possible)
1 orange, peeled (use oranges that are best for juicing and never juice citrus fruits with the skin)
1 lemon (peeled and organic if possible)
½ medium cucumber (organic if possible)
Shredded coconut (only fresh and for added sweetness and totally optional)

1. Peel the apples, orange, lemon, and cucumber.
2. Next cut and chop the fruits and veggies.
3. Put all the fruits and veggies from the ingredients list into your favorite juicer or blender or a combination of juicer/blender and strictly follow the directions of the manual that comes with your machine.
4. The manual will tell you what buttons to push and what speed to use.
5. Juice the softer textures first.
6. You will see that when you are juicing the crunchier veggies and fruits they will help you push the softer and more delicate fruits and veggies through the blades.
7. If you are not using a juicer and only have a blender available, make sure to first strain the juice from the orange and lemon.
8. Once it is finished you can either leave the pulp inside or take it out. This is totally up to your preference.
9. In this case you have to add the juice back to the blender and proceed from there.
10. Juice and blend the juices with the other ingredients from the list above together as per instructions.
11. You can always add some raw honey or sweetener depending on your goal with these juices. If the juice is too strong for you, you might also add some ice cubes or source water.
12. Enjoy

PER SERVING

Calories: 967 | Fat: 6g | Protein: 29g | Carbohydrates: 228g | Sugar: 145g

Carroty Radish Cleanser
Prep time: 10 minutes | Cook time: 0 minutes | Serves 1

1 Apple (organic if possible)
5 carrots (organic if possible)
1 beet (organic if possible)
1 cucumber (organic if possible)
1 black radish (organic if possible)

1. Peel the apple, the radish, the beets (or buy them already prepared and ready to use), carrots and cucumber.
2. Next cut and chop the veggies.
3. Put all the veggies from the ingredients list into your favorite juicer or blender or a combination of juicer/blender and strictly follow the directions of the manual that comes with your machine.
4. The manual will tell you what buttons to push and what speed to use.
5. Juice the softer textures first. You will see that when you are juicing the crunchier fruits and veggies first they will help you push the softer and more delicate ones through the blades.
6. Juice and blend all the ingredients from the list above together as per instructions.
7. Enjoy this refreshing and hydrating Beet and Black Radish Liver Cleanser!

PER SERVING

Calories: 316 | Fat: 2g | Protein: 8g | Carbohydrates: 77g | Sugar: 46g

Carroty Beet Trianon with Apple
Prep time: 10 minutes | Cook time: 0 minutes | Serves 1

2 Carrot (organic if possible)
1 Apple (organic if possible)
6 Celery Ribs (organic if possible)
1 Beet (small and organic if possible)
1 hand full of cilantro and/or parsley and/or cilantro
1" size slice of ginger (organic if possible)

1. Peel the beets (or buy them already prepared and ready to use), apple, carrots and ginger.
2. Next cut and chop the fruits and veggies.
3. Put all the fruits and veggies from the ingredients list into your favorite juicer or blender or a combination of juicer/blender and strictly follow the directions of the manual that comes with your machine.
4. Juice the softer fruits/textures first.
5. You will see that when you are juicing the crunchier veggies and fruits they will help you push the softer and more delicate fruits and veggies through the blades.
6. Juice and blend all the ingredients from the list above together as per instructions.
7. You can always add some raw honey or sweetener depending on your goal with these juices. If the juice is too strong for you, you might also add some ice cubes or source water.
8. Enjoy the Apple Carrot Beet Trianon!

PER SERVING

Calories: 168 | Fat: 1g | Protein: 3g | Carbohydrates: 42g | Sugar: 28g

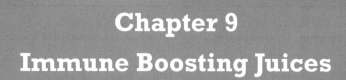

Chapter 9
Immune Boosting Juices

Cinnamon Anti-Inflammatory Juice

Prep time: 10 minutes | Cook time: 0 minutes | Serves 1

1 cup spinach
4 carrots
2 celery ribs
1 green apple
½ teaspoon ground cinnamon

1. Wash the spinach, carrots, celery, and apple.
2. Trim the ends from the carrots and celery, then cut into 4-inch pieces.
3. Remove the apple core and discard. Cut the apple into quarters, leaving the peel intact.
4. Place a pitcher under the juicer's spout to collect the juice.
5. Feed the first four ingredients through the juicer's intake tube in the order listed.
6. When the juice stops flowing, remove the pitcher, add the cinnamon, and stir the juice.
7. Serve immediately.

PER SERVING

Calories: 106| Fat: 1g | Protein: 3g | Carbohydrates: 33g | Sugar: 20g

Garlicky Cabbage with Carrot and Lemon

Prep time: 15 minutes | Cook time: 0 minutes | Serves 1

1½ cucumbers
2 cups spinach
½ cup green cabbage
3 carrots
1 garlic clove, peeled
1 lemon

1. Wash all the ingredients except the garlic.
2. Trim the ends from the cucumbers and carrots, then cut into 4-inch pieces.
3. Cut the cabbage in half, then slice or chop into smaller pieces.
4. Peel the lemon and cut into quarters.
5. Place a pitcher under the juicer's spout to collect the juice.
6. Feed each ingredient through the juicer's intake tube in the order listed.
7. When the juice stops flowing, remove the pitcher and stir the juice.
8. Serve immediately.

PER SERVING

Calories: 121| Fat: 1g | Protein: 6g | Carbohydrates: 41g | Sugar: 16g

Immune Boosting Green Mix

Prep time: 15 minutes | Cook time: 0 minutes | Serves 1

2 cups kale
½ cup dandelion greens
1 pear
½ lemon

1. Wash all the ingredients.
2. Cut the pear into quarters, removing the core and seeds, but leaving the peel intact.
3. Peel the lemon half and cut into quarters.
4. Place a pitcher under the juicer's spout to collect the juice.
5. Feed each ingredient through the juicer's intake tube in the order listed.
6. When the juice stops flowing, remove the pitcher and stir the juice.
7. Serve immediately.

PER SERVING

Calories: 162| Fat: 2g | Protein: 10g | Carbohydrates: 50g | Sugar: 22g

Spinach with Cherry Ginger Blast

Prep time: 15 minutes | Cook time: 0 minutes | Serves 1

1½ cups spinach
1 cup cherries
Fresh ginger root
1 cup sparkling water

1. Wash the spinach, cherries, and ginger root.
2. Remove the cherry pits and stems.
3. Slice off a 2-inch piece of the ginger root.
4. Place a pitcher under the juicer's spout to collect the juice.
5. Feed each ingredient through the juicer's intake tube in the order listed.
6. When the juice stops flowing, remove the pitcher and stir the juice.
7. Serve immediately.

PER SERVING

Calories: 76| Fat: 0g | Protein: 2g | Carbohydrates: 21g | Sugar: 14g

Carrot with Orange Immune Support

Prep time: 15 minutes | Cook time: 0 minutes | Serves 2

3 medium carrots
2 small oranges, peeled

1. Peel, cut, deseed, and/or chop the ingredients as needed.
1. Place a container under the juicer's spout.
2. Feed the ingredients one at a time, in the order listed, through the juicer.
3. Stir the juice and pour into glasses to serve.

PER SERVING

Calories: 75| Fat: 1g | Protein: 2g | Carbohydrates: 18g | Sugar: 9g

Broccoli with Carrot Immunity Plus

Prep time: 15 minutes | Cook time: 0 minutes | Serves 1

1 small beet
2 carrots
8 celery ribs
1 broccoli stalk
2 garlic cloves, peeled

1. Wash all the ingredients except the garlic.
2. Remove any greens from the beet and save for juicing later. Cut the beet into quarters.
3. Trim the ends from the carrots and celery, then cut into 4-inch pieces.
4. Remove the stalk from the broccoli crown with a knife and discard or save to juice later. Cut the crown into small florets.
5. Place a pitcher under the juicer's spout to collect the juice.
6. Feed each ingredient through the juicer's intake tube in the order listed.
7. When the juice stops flowing, remove the pitcher and stir the juice.
8. Serve immediately.

PER SERVING

Calories: 120| Fat: 1g | Protein: 7g | Carbohydrates: 34g | Sugar: 17g

Sprout with Aloe Cleanser

Prep time: 10 minutes | Cook time: 0 minutes | Serves 1

¼ cup alfalfa sprouts
1 pear
1 cup cabbage
¼ cup aloe vera juice

1. Wash the alfalfa sprouts, pear, and cabbage.
2. Cut the pear into quarters, removing the core and seeds, but leaving the peel intact.
3. Cut the cabbage in half, then slice or chop into smaller pieces.
4. Place a pitcher under the juicer's spout to collect the juice.
5. Feed the first three ingredients through the juicer's intake tube in the order listed.
6. When the juice stops flowing, remove the pitcher, add the aloe vera juice, and stir.
7. Serve immediately.

PER SERVING

Calories: 91| Fat: 0g | Protein: 3g | Carbohydrates: 29g | Sugar: 17g

Lemony Papaya and Kale Mix

Prep time: 15 minutes | Cook time: 0 minutes | Serves 1

1 cup papaya
6 kale leaves
Fresh turmeric root
1 lemon

1. Wash the kale, turmeric root, and lemon.
2. Cut the papaya in half lengthwise. Scoop out seeds and discard, then scoop out flesh and discard the papaya skin.
3. Slice off a 2-inch piece of the turmeric root.
4. Peel the lemon and cut into quarters.
5. Place a pitcher under the juicer's spout to collect the juice.
6. Feed each ingredient through the juicer's intake tube in the order listed.
7. When the juice stops flowing, remove the pitcher, and stir the juice.
8. Serve immediately.

PER SERVING

Calories: 127| Fat: 0g | Protein: 8g | Carbohydrates: 36g | Sugar: 14g

Spiced Broccoli with Green Leaves

Prep time: 15 minutes | Cook time: 0 minutes | Serves 1

1 orange
½ red bell pepper
1 cup broccoli
2 collard green leaves
¼ cucumber

1. Wash all the ingredients.
2. Peel the orange and cut into quarters.
3. Remove the stem and seeds from the bell pepper. Cut into small pieces.
4. Remove the stalk from the broccoli crown with a knife and discard or save to juice later. Cut the crown into small florets.
5. Trim the ends from the cucumber, then cut into quarters.
6. Place a pitcher under the juicer's spout to collect the juice.
7. Feed each ingredient through the juicer's intake tube in the order listed.
8. When the juice stops flowing, remove the pitcher and stir the juice.
9. Serve immediately.

PER SERVING

Calories: 81| Fat: 1g | Protein: 4g | Carbohydrates: 24g | Sugar: 15g

Carrot with Healthy Healing Greens
Prep time: 15 minutes | Cook time: 0 minutes | Serves 1

2 cups spinach
3 cups broccoli
4 celery ribs
2 carrots

1. Wash all the ingredients.
2. Remove the stalk from the broccoli crown with a knife and discard or save to juice later. Cut the crown into small florets.
3. Trim the ends from the celery and carrots, then cut into 4-inch pieces.
4. Place a pitcher under the juicer's spout to collect the juice.
5. Feed each ingredient through the juicer's intake tube in the order listed.
6. When the juice stops flowing, remove the pitcher and stir the juice.
7. Serve immediately.

PER SERVING

Calories: 69| Fat: 1g | Protein: 6g | Carbohydrates: 20g | Sugar: 7g

Grapy Collard with Juicy Orange Mix
Prep time: 5 minutes | Cook time: 0 minutes | Serves 2

2 medium collard leaves
1 grapefruit, peeled
2 small oranges, peeled

1. Peel, cut, deseed, and/or chop the ingredients as needed.
2. Place a container under the juicer's spout.
3. Feed the ingredients one at a time, in the order listed, through the juicer.
4. Stir the juice and pour into glasses to serve.

PER SERVING

Calories: 150| Fat: 1g | Protein: 4g | Carbohydrates: 36g | Sugar: 9g

Fruity Papaya Juice with Berries
Prep time: 10 minutes | Cook time: 0 minutes | Serves 2

1 large celery stalk
4 large romaine leaves
1 small apple
1 cup papaya
1 cup strawberries
1 cup watermelon
1. Peel, cut, deseed, and/or chop the ingredients as needed.
2. Place a container under the juicer's spout.
3. Feed the ingredients one at a time, in the order listed, through the juicer.
4. Stir the juice and pour into glasses to serve.

PER SERVING

Calories: 136| Fat: 1g | Protein: 2g | Carbohydrates: 34g | Sugar: 25g

Purple and Red Grape with Kale
Prep time: 10 minutes | Cook time: 0 minutes | Serves 2

2 large kale leaves
½ cup black, purple, or red grapes
½ cup pineapple
2 cups watermelon

1. Peel, cut, deseed, and/or chop the ingredients as needed.
2. Place a container under the juicer's spout.
3. Feed the ingredients one at a time, in the order listed, through the juicer.
4. Stir the juice and pour into glasses to serve.

PER SERVING

Calories: 257| Fat: 1g | Protein: 12g | Carbohydrates: 53g | Sugar: 20g

Limey Kale with Melon Juice
Prep time: 10 minutes | Cook time: 0 minutes | Serves 2

1 large kale leaf
1 cup mango
½ lime, peeled
2 cups watermelon
½ cup fresh coconut water

1. Peel, cut, deseed, and/or chop the ingredients as needed.
2. Place a container under the juicer's spout.
3. Feed the ingredients one at a time, in the order listed, through the juicer.
4. Stir the coconut water directly into the juice.

PER SERVING

Calories: 114| Fat: 1g | Protein: 3g | Carbohydrates: 28g | Sugar: 23g

Grapy Romaine Immune Booster
Prep time: 10 minutes | Cook time: 0 minutes | Serves 2

2 large celery stalks
4 large romaine leaves
1 pink or red grapefruit, peeled

1. Peel, cut, deseed, and/or chop the ingredients as needed.
2. Place a container under the juicer's spout.
3. Feed the ingredients one at a time, in the order listed, through the juicer.
4. Stir the juice and pour into glasses to serve.

PER SERVING

Calories: 71| Fat: 1g | Protein: 5g | Carbohydrates: 14g | Sugar: 9g

Grape with Spinach Booster Juice

Prep time: 10 minutes | Cook time: 0 minutes | Serves 2

4 cups spinach
½ pink or red grapefruit, peeled
4 cups watermelon

1. Peel, cut, deseed, and/or chop the ingredients as needed.
2. Place a container under the juicer's spout.
3. Feed the ingredients one at a time, in the order listed, through the juicer.
4. Stir the juice and pour into glasses to serve.

PER SERVING

Calories: 127| Fat: 1g | Protein: 4g | Carbohydrates: 31g | Sugar: 24g

Limey Cantaloupe Booster

Prep time: 10 minutes | Cook time: 0 minutes | Serves 2

2 limes, peeled
4 cups cantaloupe
.

1. Peel, cut, deseed, and/or chop the ingredients as needed.
2. Place a container under the juicer's spout.
3. Feed the ingredients one at a time, in the order listed, through the juicer.
4. Stir the juice and pour into glasses to serve.

PER SERVING

Calories: 131| Fat: 1g | Protein: 3g | Carbohydrates: 33g | Sugar: 29g

Cantaloupe with Rosy Carrot

Prep time: 10 minutes | Cook time: 0 minutes | Serves 2

4 medium carrots
1 cup cantaloupe

1. Peel, cut, deseed, and/or chop the ingredients as needed.
2. Place a container under the juicer's spout.
3. Feed the ingredients one at a time, in the order listed, through the juicer.
4. Stir the juice and pour into glasses to serve.

PER SERVING

Calories: 80| Fat: 1g | Protein: 2g | Carbohydrates: 19g | Sugar: 13g

Dragon Fruit with Spinach Mix

Prep time: 10 minutes | Cook time: 0 minutes | Serves 2

1 dragon fruit (pitaya)
1 small collard leaf
1 large cucumber
Handful spinach
1 small apple

1. Cut open the dragon fruit, scoop out the pulp and seeds, and discard the rind.
2. Alternate ingredients, finishing with the apple.

PER SERVING

Calories: 100| Fat: 1g | Protein: 2g | Carbohydrates: 25g | Sugar: 19g

Spicy Melon Immune Booster

Prep time: 5 minutes | Cook time: 0 minutes | Serves 2

1 large yellow bell pepper
4 cups watermelon

1. Peel, cut, deseed, and/or chop the ingredients as needed.
2. Place a container under the juicer's spout.
3. Feed the ingredients one at a time, in the order listed, through the juicer.
4. Stir the juice and pour into glasses to serve.

PER SERVING

Calories: 101| Fat: 1g | Protein: 2g | Carbohydrates: 25g | Sugar: 20g

Mango Orange Immune Booster

Prep time: 10 minutes | Cook time: 0 minutes | Serves 2

1 cup mango
1-inch piece fresh ginger root
2 oranges, peeled
½ large cucumber

1. Peel, cut, deseed, and/or chop the ingredients as needed.
2. Place a container under the juicer's spout.
3. Feed the ingredients one at a time, in the order listed, through the juicer.
4. Stir the juice and pour into glasses to serve.

PER SERVING

Calories: 318| Fat: 2g | Protein: 6g | Carbohydrates: 77g | Sugar: 25g

Mango and Orange with Arugula Boost
Prep time: 10 minutes | Cook time: 0 minutes | Serves 2

Handful arugula
1-inch piece fresh ginger root
1 lime, peeled
1 cup mango
1 orange, peeled
1 cup papaya
½ large cucumber

1. Peel, cut, deseed, and/or chop the ingredients as needed.
2. Place a container under the juicer's spout.
3. Feed the ingredients one at a time, in the order listed, through the juicer.
4. Stir the juice and pour into glasses to serve.

PER SERVING

Calories: 163| Fat: 1g | Protein: 3g | Carbohydrates: 41g | Sugar: 22g

Fruity Immune Boosting Mix
Prep time: 10 minutes | Cook time: 0 minutes | Serves 2

1 orange, peeled
1 cup papaya
1 firm pear
1-inch piece fresh ginger root
½ large cucumber

1. Peel, cut, deseed, and/or chop the ingredients as needed.
2. Place a container under the juicer's spout.
3. Feed the ingredients one at a time, in the order listed, through the juicer.
4. Stir the juice and pour into glasses to serve.

PER SERVING

Calories: 134| Fat: 1g | Protein: 2g | Carbohydrates: 33g | Sugar: 14g

Spiced Arugula with Grapy Orange
Prep time: 10 minutes | Cook time: 0 minutes | Serves 2

Handful arugula
½ yellow bell pepper
4 small kale leaves
1 cup black, purple, or red grapes
1 orange, peeled

1. Peel, cut, deseed, and/or chop the ingredients as needed.
2. Place a container under the juicer's spout.
3. Feed the ingredients one at a time, in the order listed, through the juicer.
4. Stir the juice and pour into glasses to serve.

PER SERVING

Calories: 454| Fat: 3g | Protein: 28g | Carbohydrates: 86g | Sugar: 6g

Melony Cauliflower Power
Prep time: 5 minutes | Cook time: 0 minutes | Serves 2

½ cup cauliflower
4 large celery stalks
2 cups watermelon

1. Peel, cut, deseed, and/or chop the ingredients as needed.
2. Place a container under the juicer's spout.
3. Feed the ingredients one at a time, in the order listed, through the juicer.
4. Stir the juice and pour into glasses to serve.

PER SERVING

Calories: 58| Fat: 1g | Protein: 2g | Carbohydrates: 14g | Sugar: 11g

Spicy Lemon with Spinach Blend
Prep time: 10 minutes | Cook time: 0 minutes | Serves 2

2 large yellow bell peppers
4 cups spinach
1 lemon
½ large cucumber

1. Peel, cut, deseed, and/or chop the ingredients as needed.
2. Place a container under the juicer's spout.
3. Feed the ingredients one at a time, in the order listed, through the juicer.
4. Stir the juice and pour into glasses to serve.

PER SERVING

Calories: 45| Fat: 1g | Protein: 3g | Carbohydrates: 10g | Sugar: 4g

Gingered Berry with Kiwi Cooler
Prep time: 10 minutes | Cook time: 0 minutes | Serves 2

2 cups kiwifruit
2 cups mango
1 cup strawberries
1-inch piece fresh ginger root
4 medium celery stalks

1. Peel, cut, deseed, and/or chop the ingredients as needed.
2. Place a container under the juicer's spout.
3. Feed the ingredients one at a time, in the order listed, through the juicer.
4. Stir the juice and pour into glasses to serve.

PER SERVING

Calories: 238| Fat: 2g | Protein: 4g | Carbohydrates: 58g | Sugar: 43g

Spicy Kiwi with Ginger and Orange
Prep time: 10 minutes | Cook time: 0 minutes | Serves 2

1 large yellow bell pepper
2-inch piece fresh ginger root
2 kiwifruits
2 oranges, peeled

1. Peel, cut, deseed, and/or chop the ingredients as needed.
2. Place a container under the juicer's spout.
3. Feed the ingredients one at a time, in the order listed, through the juicer.
4. Stir the juice and pour into glasses to serve.

PER SERVING

Calories: 153| Fat: 1g | Protein: 3g | Carbohydrates: 37g | Sugar: 7g

Pear and Cucumber with Orchard Kiwi
Prep time: 10 minutes | Cook time: 0 minutes | Serves 2

2 kiwifruits
2 firm pears
½ large cucumber

1. Peel, cut, deseed, and/or chop the ingredients as needed.
2. Place a container under the juicer's spout.
3. Feed the ingredients one at a time, in the order listed, through the juicer.
4. Stir the juice and pour into glasses to serve.

PER SERVING

Calories: 102| Fat: 1g | Protein: 2g | Carbohydrates: 25g | Sugar: 16g

Ginger with Carrot-Infused Juice
Prep time: 10 minutes | Cook time: 0 minutes | Serves 2

2-inch piece fresh ginger root
4 kiwifruits
1 lemon
8 medium carrots

1. Peel, cut, deseed, and/or chop the ingredients as needed.
2. Place a container under the juicer's spout.
3. Feed the ingredients one at a time, in the order listed, through the juicer.
4. Stir the juice and pour into glasses to serve.

PER SERVING

Calories: 191| Fat: 1g | Protein: 4g | Carbohydrates: 46g | Sugar: 25g

Spiced Papaya with Kiwifruit
Prep time: 5 minutes | Cook time: 0 minutes | Serves 2

1 large yellow bell pepper
2 kiwifruits
1 cup papaya
1 orange, peeled

1. Peel, cut, deseed, and/or chop the ingredients as needed.
2. Place a container under the juicer's spout.
3. Feed the ingredients one at a time, in the order listed, through the juicer.
4. Stir the juice and pour into glasses to serve.

PER SERVING

Calories: 151| Fat: 1g | Protein: 3g | Carbohydrates: 37g | Sugar: 16g

Papaya with Limey Kiwi Mix
Prep time: 10 minutes | Cook time: 0 minutes | Serves 2

2 cups papaya
2 kiwifruits
1 lime, peeled
2 cups cantaloupe

1. Peel, cut, deseed, and/or chop the ingredients as needed.
2. Place a container under the juicer's spout.
3. Feed the ingredients one at a time, in the order listed, through the juicer.
4. Stir the juice and pour into glasses to serve.

PER SERVING

Calories: 207| Fat: 1g | Protein: 4g | Carbohydrates: 51g | Sugar: 38g

Melony Broccoli and Pineapple Treat
Prep time: 5 minutes | Cook time: 0 minutes | Serves 2

½ cup broccoli stems
1 cup pineapple
4 cups watermelon

1. Peel, cut, deseed, and/or chop the ingredients as needed.
2. Place a container under the juicer's spout.
3. Feed the ingredients one at a time, in the order listed, through the juicer.
4. Stir the juice and pour into glasses to serve.

PER SERVING

Calories: 169| Fat: 1g | Protein: 3g | Carbohydrates: 44g | Sugar: 37g

Cucumber with Spicy Citrus Juice
Prep time: 5 minutes | Cook time: 0 minutes | Serves 2

½ large yellow bell pepper
1 pink or red grapefruit, peeled
2 cups strawberries
½ large cucumber

1. Peel, cut, deseed, and/or chop the ingredients as needed.
2. Place a container under the juicer's spout.
3. Feed the ingredients one at a time, in the order listed, through the juicer.
4. Stir the juice and pour into glasses to serve.

PER SERVING

Calories: 100| Fat: 1g | Protein: 3g | Carbohydrates: 24g | Sugar: 17g

Arugula with Kale Booster Juice
Prep time: 5 minutes | Cook time: 0 minutes | Serves 2

½ cup arugula
2 medium kale leaves
1 orange, peeled
2 cups pineapple

1. Peel, cut, deseed, and/or chop the ingredients as needed.
2. Place a container under the juicer's spout.
3. Feed the ingredients one at a time, in the order listed, through the juicer.
4. Stir the juice and pour into glasses to serve.

PER SERVING

Calories: 209| Fat: 1g | Protein: 3g | Carbohydrates: 53g | Sugar: 37g

Immune Boosting Orange-Ginger Shot
Prep time: 5 minutes | Cook time: 0 minutes | Serves 1

½- to 1-inch piece fresh ginger root
1 small orange, peeled

1. Peel, cut, deseed, and/or chop the ingredients as needed.
2. Place a container under the juicer's spout.
3. Feed the ingredients one at a time, in the order listed, through the juicer.
4. Stir the juice and pour into glasses to serve.

PER SERVING

Calories: 101| Fat: 1g | Protein: 2g | Carbohydrates: 25g | Sugar: 0g

Spiced Ginger Shot
Prep time: 5 minutes | Cook time: 0 minutes | Serves 2

½- to 1-inch piece fresh ginger root
¼ large yellow bell pepper
¼ lemon
2-inch piece celery

1. Peel, cut, deseed, and/or chop the ingredients as needed.
2. Place a container under the juicer's spout.
3. Feed the ingredients one at a time, in the order listed, through the juicer.
4. Stir the juice and pour into glasses to serve.

PER SERVING

Calories: 4| Fat: 0g | Protein: 0g | Carbohydrates: 1g | Sugar: 1g

Lemony Bell Pepper Boost
Prep time: 5 minutes | Cook time: 0 minutes | Serves 3

2 large yellow bell peppers
1 large celery stalk
1 lemon
1-inch piece fresh ginger root
1 pink or red grapefruit, peeled

1. Peel, cut, deseed, and/or chop the ingredients as needed.
2. Place a container under the juicer's spout.
3. Feed the ingredients one at a time, in the order listed, through the juicer.
4. Stir the juice and pour into glasses to serve.

PER SERVING

Calories: 44| Fat: 0g | Protein: 1g | Carbohydrates: 11g | Sugar: 8g

Spinach with Pear-Grapefruit Cooler
Prep time: 5 minutes | Cook time: 0 minutes | Serves 1

4 medium celery stalks
½ large cucumber
Handful spinach
1 firm pear
½ pink or red grapefruit, peeled
1 cup pineapple

1. Peel, cut, deseed, and/or chop the ingredients as needed.
2. Place a container under the juicer's spout.
3. Feed the ingredients one at a time, in the order listed, through the juicer.
4. Stir the juice and pour into glasses to serve.

PER SERVING

Calories: 335| Fat: 0g | Protein: 12g | Carbohydrates: 78g | Sugar: 58g

Asparagus And Kale Salad
Prep time: 5 minutes | Cook time: 0 minutes | Serves 2

8 asparagus spears
½ lemon
4 medium kale leaves
4 small carrots
8 small celery stalks
1 large cucumber

1. Peel, cut, deseed, and/or chop the ingredients as needed.
2. Place a container under the juicer's spout.
3. Feed the ingredients one at a time, in the order listed, through the juicer.
4. Stir the juice and pour into glasses to serve.

PER SERVING

Calories: 90| Fat: 1g | Protein: 4g | Carbohydrates: 19g | Sugar: 9g

Romaine with Strawberry Juicy Boost
Prep time: 5 minutes | Cook time: 0 minutes | Serves 2

1 large carrot
1 cup strawberries
8 medium romaine leaves
8 small celery stalks

1. Peel, cut, deseed, and/or chop the ingredients as needed.
2. Place a container under the juicer's spout.
3. Feed the ingredients one at a time, in the order listed, through the juicer.
4. Stir the juice and pour into glasses to serve.

PER SERVING

Calories: 102| Fat: 2g | Protein: 9g | Carbohydrates: 18g | Sugar: 6g

Beet with Lemony Celery Booster
Prep time: 5 minutes | Cook time: 0 minutes | Serves 2

1 medium golden or red beet
1 large yellow bell pepper
1-inch piece fresh ginger root
½ lemon
8 small celery stalks
½ large cucumber

1. Peel, cut, deseed, and/or chop the ingredients as needed.
2. Place a container under the juicer's spout.
3. Feed the ingredients one at a time, in the order listed, through the juicer.
4. Stir the juice and pour into glasses to serve.

PER SERVING

Calories: 49| Fat: 1g | Protein: 2g | Carbohydrates: 11g | Sugar: 6g

Cucumber Blend with Spicy Chard
Prep time: 5 minutes | Cook time: 0 minutes | Serves 2

8 asparagus spears
2 cups Swiss chard
½ lemon
1 orange, peeled
½ yellow bell pepper
1 large cucumber

1. Peel, cut, deseed, and/or chop the ingredients as needed.
2. Place a container under the juicer's spout.
3. Feed the ingredients one at a time, in the order listed, through the juicer.
4. Stir the juice and pour into glasses to serve.

PER SERVING

Calories: 84| Fat: 1g | Protein: 3g | Carbohydrates: 19g | Sugar: 4g

Carrot And Celery for Healthy Cells
Prep time: 5 minutes | Cook time: 0 minutes | Serves 2

4 large carrots
½ lemon
6 large celery stalks

1. Peel, cut, deseed, and/or chop the ingredients as needed.
2. Place a container under the juicer's spout.
3. Feed the ingredients one at a time, in the order listed, through the juicer.
4. Stir the juice and pour into glasses to serve.

PER SERVING

Calories: 70| Fat: 1g | Protein: 2g | Carbohydrates: 16g | Sugar: 8g

Cucumber Chard Immune Support
Prep time: 5 minutes | Cook time: 0 minutes | Serves 2

8 small celery stalks
4 cups Swiss chard
2 oranges, peeled
½ large cucumber

1. Peel, cut, deseed, and/or chop the ingredients as needed.
2. Place a container under the juicer's spout.
3. Feed the ingredients one at a time, in the order listed, through the juicer.
4. Stir the juice and pour into glasses to serve.

PER SERVING

Calories: 133| Fat: 1g | Protein: 4g | Carbohydrates: 31g | Sugar: 3g

Chard with Juicy Pear Boost

Prep time: 5 minutes | Cook time: 0 minutes | Serves 2

4 small celery stalks
4 small Swiss chard leaves
1 firm pear
½ lemon
½ large cucumber

1. Peel, cut, deseed, and/or chop the ingredients as needed.
2. Place a container under the juicer's spout.
3. Feed the ingredients one at a time, in the order listed, through the juicer.
4. Stir the juice and pour into glasses to serve.

PER SERVING

Calories: 60| Fat: 1g | Protein: 3g | Carbohydrates: 14g | Sugar: 7g

Carroty Fighter Drink

Prep time: 5 minutes | Cook time: 0 minutes | Serves 1

1 beet raw
1 carrot raw
1 radish raw
½ potato raw
1 celery stalk raw

1. Wash off the vegetables properly and then juice them. The potato should be juiced with the skin. If there are any green spots, cut them off.
2. After preparing the juice pour into a glass and serve.
3. Enjoy!

PER SERVING

Calories: 266 | Fat: 1g | Protein: 8g | Carbohydrates: 60g | Sugar: 19mg

Kiwi Juice with Orange

Prep time: 5 minutes | Cook time: 0 minutes | Serves 1

2 Oranges
2 Kiwi fruits
1 medium sized Papaya

1. If you love a slight bitter taste to add to the tradition of healthy juices, then taking the whole papaya along with the seeds and skin is advisable. Juice the whole of it in a juicer. The juice is filled with array of nutrients.
2. For oranges, cut them in thin slices discarding only the orange skin and leaving behind the white pith as best as you can. The antioxidant rich pith lessens asthma's risk and is immensely useful during Hay Fever. This amazing combination supports eye strength as well.
3. Combine all the ingredients in a juicer and serve chilled.
4. Enjoy!

PER SERVING

Calories: 536 | Fat: 3g | Protein: 8g | Carbohydrates: 134g | Sugar: 61mg

Milky Sweet Potato Pear Juice

Prep time: 5 minutes | Cook time: 0 minutes | Serves 1
Two cups chopped sweet potato
Three pears, core removed and chopped
One cup coconut milk

1. Rinse off the sweet potato and pear.
2. Juice the sweet potato and pear.
3. Stir in the coconut milk.
4. Serve room temperature.

PER SERVING

Calories: 305 | Fat: 6g | Protein: 0g | Carbohydrates: 45g | Sugar: 25mg

Fruity Kaki Drink

Prep time: 10 minutes | Cook time: 0 minutes | Serves 1
Four kaki fruits, skin removed
One orange, peeled

1. Rinse off the fruit.
1. Juice the kaki fruit and orange.
2. Serve with ice or chill in the fridge, or enjoy room temperature.

PER SERVING

Calories: 263 | Fat: 0g | Protein: 0g | Carbohydrates: 47g | Sugar: 42g

Litchi Exotic Delight

Prep time: 10 minutes | Cook time: 0 minutes | Serves 1
Three cups litchi fruit, pits removed, and outer shell removed
One cup coconut water

1. Rinse off the litchi fruit.
2. Juice the litchis.
3. Stir in the coconut water.

PER SERVING

Calories: 189 | Fat: 0g | Protein: 0g | Carbohydrates: 33g | Sugar: 71g

Fruity Cosmic Juice

Prep time: 10 minutes | Cook time: 0 minutes | Serves 1
One dragon fruit, skin removed and cut into small pieces
Two starfruits, skin removed, chopped
One cup coconut water

1. Rinse off the fruit.
2. Juice the star fruit and dragon fruit.
4. Stir in the coconut water.
3. Serve with ice or chill in the fridge, or enjoy room temperature.

PER SERVING

Calories: 120 | Fat: 0g | Protein: 0g | Carbohydrates: 29g | Sugar: 10g

Tropical Orange & Banana Juice
Prep time: 10 minutes | Cook time: 0 minutes | Serves 1

2 oranges, peeled
1 banana, peeled
1 cup coconut water

1. Rinse off the oranges.
2. Juice the oranges.
3. Place the orange juice along with the banana and the coconut water in a blender.
4. Blend and serve with ice or room temperature, or chill in the fridge.

PER SERVING

Calories: 200 | Fat: 0.5g | Protein: 0g | Carbohydrates: 43g | Sugar: 38g

Milky Coconut Berry Swirl
Prep time: 10 minutes | Cook time: 0 minutes | Serves 1

3 cup raspberries
1 cup coconut milk
1 cup coconut water

1. Rinse off the raspberries.
2. Stir in the coconut milk and coconut water.
3. Serve with ice or chill in the fridge, or enjoy room temperature.

PER SERVING

Calories: 280 | Fat: 7g | Protein: 0g | Carbohydrates: 40g | Sugar: 172g

Blood Orange Booster
Prep time: 10 minutes | Cook time: 0 minutes | Serves 1

2 blood oranges, peeled
Quarter of pineapple
1 big banana
A couple of ice

1. Peel the oranges, leave the white pith.
2. Juice the oranges and pineapple.
3. Pour the juice with peeled banana and ice into the blender.
4. Blend.
5. This drink can provide a quick energy boost, making you more alert and also helps to regulate blood sugar level.

PER SERVING

Calories: 224 | Fat: 0g | Protein: 0g | Carbohydrates: 29g | Sugar: 25g

Body Dew Juice
Prep time: 10 minutes | Cook time: 0 minutes | Serves 1

One cup of blackberry
One kiwi
One medium size pear
Peppermint as optional
Quarter of peeled and cored pineapple

1. Peel and core the pineapple.
2. Juice everything.
3. Stir or shake extracted juice.
4. Serve.

PER SERVING

Calories: 209 | Fat: 1.2g | Protein: 5g | Carbohydrates: 56g | Sugar: 42g

Limey Tropical Fiesta
Prep time: 10 minutes | Cook time: 0 minutes | Serves 1

2 apples
4 kale leaves
$\frac{1}{2}$ of a peeled lime
$\frac{1}{2}$ a cup of cold coconut water

1. Wash all fruits.
2. Peel the lime.
3. Juice kale, lime and apples with a juicer.
4. Pour extracted juice in a glass with cold coconut water.
6. Serve.

PER SERVING

Calories: 174 | Fat: 1g | Protein: 3g | Carbohydrates: 73g | Sugar: 45g

Lime with Gingery Sensation
Prep time: 10 minutes | Cook time: 0 minutes | Serves 1

3 medium apples
2 big sticks of celery
1 cucumber
1 ginger root thumb
1 lime

1. Peel the lime as optional.
2. Process everything through a juicer.
3. Shake achieved juice.
4. Drink.

PER SERVING

Calories: 221 | Fat: 1g | Protein: 4g | Carbohydrates: 70g | Sugar: 60g

Chapter 10
Anti-Aging and Energizing Juices

Parsley with Limey Energy Juice
Prep time: 5 minutes | Cook time: 0 minutes | Serves 2

1 medium navel orange
1 medium apple
1 medium pear
½ bunch parsley
½ lime

1. Peel, cut, deseed, and/or chop the ingredients as needed.
2. Place a container under the juicer's spout.
3. Feed the ingredients one at a time, in the order listed, through the juicer.
4. Stir the juice and pour into glasses to serve.

PER SERVING

Calories: 115 | Fat: 1g | Protein: 2g | Carbohydrates: 30g | Sugar: 20g

Lemony Berry Renewal Juice
Prep time: 5 minutes | Cook time: 0 minutes | Serves 2

2 cups raspberries
1 large carrot
1 medium pear
1 tablespoon freshly squeezed lemon juice

1. Peel, cut, deseed, and/or chop the ingredients as needed.
2. Place a container under the juicer's spout.
3. Feed the raspberries, carrot, and pear through the juicer.
4. Stir the lemon juice into the juice and pour into glasses to serve.

PER SERVING

Calories: 275| Fat: 1g | Protein: 3g | Carbohydrates: 70g | Sugar: 58g

Spicy Beet and Apple Power Juice
Prep time: 5 minutes | Cook time: 0 minutes | Serves 2

2 medium apples
2 small beets
1 large, sweet potato
1 large carrot
1 small red bell pepper

1. Peel, cut, deseed, and/or chop the ingredients as needed.
2. Place a container under the juicer's spout.
3. Feed the ingredients one at a time, in the order listed, through the juicer.
4. Stir the juice and pour into glasses to serve.

PER SERVING

Calories: 349| Fat: 1g | Protein: 5g | Carbohydrates: 86g | Sugar: 59g

Celery with Parsley Power Juice
Prep time: 5 minutes | Cook time: 0 minutes | Serves 2

1 bunch parsley leaves
2 medium carrots
2 large stalks celery
1 small apple

1. Peel, cut, deseed, and/or chop the ingredients as needed.
2. Place a container under the juicer's spout.
3. Feed the ingredients one at a time, in the order listed, through the juicer.
4. Stir the juice and pour into glasses to serve.

PER SERVING

Calories: 77| Fat: 1g | Protein: 2g | Carbohydrates: 19g | Sugar: 11g

Collards with Kale Power Juice
Prep time: 5 minutes | Cook time: 0 minutes | Serves 2
1 bunch kale leaves
1 small head broccoli
1 large stalk celery
½ bunch collard greens
1 tablespoon hempseed

1. Peel, cut, deseed, and/or chop the ingredients as needed.
2. Place a container under the juicer's spout.
3. Feed the first four ingredients one at a time, in the order listed, through the juicer.
4. Stir the hempseed into the juice and pour into glasses to serve.

PER SERVING

Calories: 25| Fat: 1g | Protein: 3g | Carbohydrates: 4g | Sugar: 1g

Lemony Spinach with Gingered Pear
Prep time: 5 minutes | Cook time: 0 minutes | Serves 1
1 pear
3 cups baby spinach
1 cucumber
½ lemon
Fresh ginger root

1. Wash all the ingredients.
2. Cut the pear into quarters, removing the core and seeds, but leaving the peel intact.
3. Trim the ends from the cucumber, then cut into 4-inch pieces.
4. Peel the lemon and cut into quarters.
5. Slice off a ½-inch piece of the ginger root.
6. Place a pitcher under the juicer's spout to collect the juice.
7. Feed each ingredient through the juicer's intake tube in the order listed.
8. Serve immediately.

PER SERVING

Calories: 135| Fat: 1g | Protein: 5g | Carbohydrates: 44g | Sugar: 21mg

Limey Green Skin-Healing Juice

Prep time: 5 minutes | Cook time: 0 minutes | Serves 1

2 cups spinach
3 kale leaves
½ cucumber
1 green apple
2 tablespoons cilantro sprigs
½ lime
Fresh ginger root

1. Wash all the ingredients.
2. Trim the ends from the cucumber, then cut into 4-inch pieces.
3. Remove the apple core and discard. Cut the apple into quarters, leaving the peel intact.
4. Peel the lime and cut into quarters.
5. Slice off a ½-inch piece of the ginger root.
6. Place a pitcher under the juicer's spout to collect the juice.
7. Feed each ingredient through the juicer's intake tube in the order listed.
8. When the juice stops flowing, remove the pitcher and stir the juice.
9. Serve immediately.

PER SERVING

Calories: 103| Fat: 1g | Protein: 4g | Carbohydrates: 31g | Sugar: 16mg

Lemony Detox Juice

Prep time: 5 minutes | Cook time: 0 minutes | Serves 1

1 cup spinach
1 cup cubed sweet potato
3 celery ribs
1 zucchini
1 cucumber
½ lemon

1. Wash all the ingredients.
2. Peel the sweet potato and cut into small cubes.
3. Trim the ends from the celery, zucchini, and cucumber, then cut into 4-inch pieces.
4. Peel the lemon half and cut into quarters.
5. Place a pitcher under the juicer's spout to collect the juice.
6. Feed each ingredient through the juicer's intake tube in the order listed.
7. When the juice stops flowing, remove the pitcher and stir the juice.
8. Serve immediately.

PER SERVING

Calories: 123| Fat: 1g | Protein: 5g | Carbohydrates: 34g | Sugar: 11mg

Carrot with Celery Juice

Prep time: 5 minutes | Cook time: 0 minutes | Serves 1

6 carrots
1 romaine heart
2 celery ribs
1 orange
Fresh ginger root
Fresh turmeric root

1. Wash all the ingredients.
2. Trim the ends from the carrots and celery, then cut into 4-inch pieces.
3. Peel the orange and cut into quarters.
4. Slice off ½-inch pieces of the ginger root and the turmeric root.
5. Place a pitcher under the juicer's spout to collect the juice.
6. Feed each ingredient through the juicer's intake tube in the order listed.
7. When the juice stops flowing, remove the pitcher and stir the juice.
8. Serve immediately.

PER SERVING

Calories: 151| Fat: 2g | Protein: 7g | Carbohydrates: 46g | Sugar: 24mg

Berry with Kale and Celery Juice

Prep time: 5 minutes | Cook time: 0 minutes | Serves 1

6 strawberries
6 kale leaves
2 celery ribs
½ cucumber

1. Wash all the ingredients.
2. Trim the ends from the celery and cucumber, then cut into 4-inch pieces.
3. Place a pitcher under the juicer's spout to collect the juice.
4. Feed each ingredient through the juicer's intake tube in the order listed.
5. When the juice stops flowing, remove the pitcher and stir the juice.
6. Serve immediately.

PER SERVING

Calories: 84| Fat: 2g | Protein: 8g | Carbohydrates: 22g | Sugar: 8mg

Artichoke with Spinach Anti-Aging Juice

Prep time: 5 minutes | Cook time: 0 minutes | Serves 1

1 artichoke
1 green apple
1 cup spinach
1 celery rib

1. Wash all the ingredients.
2. Prepare the artichoke per the instructions in the Preparation Tip.
3. Remove the apple core and discard. Cut the apple into quarters, leaving the peel intact.
4. Trim the ends from the celery, then cut into 4-inch pieces.
5. Place a pitcher under the juicer's spout to collect the juice. Then, feed each ingredient through the juicer's intake tube in the order listed.
6. When the juice stops flowing, remove the pitcher and stir the juice.
7. Serve immediately.

PER SERVING

Calories: 75| Fat: 0g | Protein: 4g | Carbohydrates: 25g | Sugar: 12mg

Kiwi Power Juice

Prep time: 5 minutes | Cook time: 0 minutes | Serves 1

4 kiwis
4 cups spinach
1 cucumber
1 lime
Pinch sea salt

1. Wash the kiwis, spinach, cucumber, and lime.
2. Trim the ends from the cucumber, then cut into 4-inch pieces.
3. Peel the kiwis and lime and cut them into quarters.
4. Place a pitcher under the juicer's spout to collect the juice.
5. Feed the first four ingredients through the juicer's intake tube in the order listed.
6. When the juice stops flowing, remove the pitcher, add the sea salt, and stir the juice.
7. Serve immediately.

PER SERVING

Calories: 145| Fat: 2g | Protein: 6g | Carbohydrates: 43g | Sugar: 22mg

Lemony Skin Clearing Juice

Prep time: 5 minutes | Cook time: 0 minutes | Serves 1

8 carrots
4 mustard green leaves
3 lemons
2 cups broccoli
Fresh turmeric root

1. Wash all the ingredients.
2. Trim the ends from the carrots, then cut into 4-inch pieces.
3. Peel the lemons and cut into quarters.
4. Remove the stalk from the broccoli crown with a knife and discard or save to juice later. Cut the crown into small florets.
5. Slice off a 2-inch piece of the turmeric root.
6. Place a pitcher under the juicer's spout to collect the juice.
7. Feed each ingredient through the juicer's intake tube in the order listed.
8. When the juice stops flowing, remove the pitcher and stir the juice.
9. Serve immediately.

PER SERVING

Calories: 171| Fat: 2g | Protein: 9g | Carbohydrates: 55g | Sugar: 22mg

Blackberry Power Green Juice

Prep time: 5 minutes | Cook time: 0 minutes | Serves 1

½ cup blackberries
4 large collard green leaves
½ lime
8 ounces sparkling mineral water

1. Wash the blackberries, collard greens, and lime.
2. Peel the lime and cut into quarters.
3. Feed the first three ingredients through the juicer's intake tube in the order listed.
4. When the juice stops flowing, remove the pitcher, add the mineral water, and stir the juice.
5. Serve immediately.

PER SERVING

Calories: 30| Fat: 1g | Protein: 3g | Carbohydrates: 12g | Sugar: 3mg

Anti-aging Supreme Juice

Prep time: 5 minutes | Cook time: 0 minutes | Serves 1

4 kale leaves
½ cup blackberries
½ green apple
1 cup broccoli
1 cucumber
½ fennel bulb

1. Wash all the ingredients.
2. Remove the apple core and discard. Cut the apple into quarters, leaving the peel intact.
3. Remove the stalk from the broccoli crown with a knife and discard or save to juice later. Cut the crown into small florets.
4. Trim the ends from the cucumber, then cut into 4-inch pieces.
5. Remove the stalks and fronds from the fennel and save for later. Cut the bulb into quarters.
6. Place a pitcher under the juicer's spout to collect the juice.
7. Feed each ingredient through the juicer's intake tube in the order listed.
8. When the juice stops flowing, remove the pitcher and stir the juice.
9. Serve immediately.

PER SERVING

Calories: 138| Fat: 2g | Protein: 10g | Carbohydrates: 41g | Sugar: 18mg

Lettuce with Grapes and Cucumber

Prep time: 5 minutes | Cook time: 0 minutes | Serves 1

3 Swiss chard leaves
3 romaine lettuce leaves
1 cup green grapes
1½ cucumbers

1. Wash all the ingredients.
2. Trim the ends from the cucumbers, then cut into 4-inch pieces.
3. Place a pitcher under the juicer's spout to collect the juice.
4. Feed each ingredient through the juicer's intake tube in the order listed.
5. When the juice stops flowing, remove the pitcher and stir the juice.
6. Serve immediately.

PER SERVING

Calories: 128| Fat: 1g | Protein: 5g | Carbohydrates: 36g | Sugar: 23mg

Spicy Celery with Tomatillo Juice

Prep time: 5 minutes | Cook time: 0 minutes | Serves 1

2 tomatillos
1 cucumber
¼ cup cilantro sprigs
2 celery ribs
½ jalapeño pepper
½ lime
½ cup pineapple juice

1. Wash all the produce.
2. Peel the outer leaf away from the tomatillos, then cut into quarters.
3. Trim the ends from the cucumber and celery, then cut into 4-inch pieces.
4. Remove the stem and seeds from the jalapeño.
5. Peel the lime and cut into quarters.
6. Place a pitcher under the juicer's spout to collect the juice.
7. Feed the first six ingredients through the juicer's intake tube in the order listed.
8. When the juice stops flowing, remove the pitcher, add the pineapple juice, and stir.
9. Serve immediately.

PER SERVING

Calories: 119| Fat: 1g | Protein: 4g | Carbohydrates: 16g | Sugar: 13mg

Coconut Berry Power Juice

Prep time: 5 minutes | Cook time: 0 minutes | Serves 1

2 cups spinach
6 celery ribs
1 cup blueberries
8 ounces coconut water

1. Wash the spinach, celery, and blueberries.
2. Trim the ends from the celery, then cut into 4-inch pieces.
3. Place a pitcher under the juicer's spout to collect the juice.
4. Feed the first three ingredients through the juicer's intake tube in the order listed.
5. When the juice stops flowing, remove the pitcher, add the coconut water, and stir.
6. Serve immediately.

PER SERVING

Calories: 73| Fat: 1g | Protein: 3g | Carbohydrates: 21g | Sugar: 13mg

Orange with Wheatgrass Power Juice
Prep time: 5 minutes | Cook time: 0 minutes | Serves 1

1 cucumber
2 cups spinach
1 handful wheatgrass
1 orange
1 green apple

1. Wash all the ingredients.
2. Trim the ends from the cucumber, then cut into 4-inch pieces.
3. Peel the orange and cut into quarters.
4. Remove the apple core and discard. Cut the apple into quarters, leaving the peel intact.
5. Place a pitcher under the juicer's spout to collect the juice.
6. Feed each ingredient through the juicer's intake tube in the order listed.
7. When the juice stops flowing, remove the pitcher and stir the juice.
8. Serve immediately.

PER SERVING
Calories: 133| Fat: 1g | Protein: 6g | Carbohydrates: 34g | Sugar: 23mg

Spinach Berry with Green Tea Juice
Prep time: 5 minutes | Cook time: 0 minutes | Serves 1

¾ cup green tea
2 cups spinach
1 red apple
2 teaspoons ground flax seed

1. Brew the green tea and let it cool.
2. Wash the spinach and apple.
3. Remove the apple core and discard. Cut the apple into quarters, leaving the peel intact.
4. Place a pitcher under the juicer's spout to collect the juice.
5. Feed the spinach, then the apple through the juicer's intake tube.
6. When the juice stops flowing, remove the pitcher, add the green tea and flax seed, then stir.
7. Serve immediately.

PER SERVING
Calories: 66| Fat: 2g | Protein: 2g | Carbohydrates: 17g | Sugar: 11mg

Minty Parsley with Ginger and Carrot
Prep time: 5 minutes | Cook time: 0 minutes | Serves 1

2 cucumbers
3 carrots
2 tablespoons parsley
1 sprig mint leaves
Fresh ginger root

1. Wash all the ingredients.
2. Trim the ends from the cucumbers and carrots, then cut into 4-inch pieces.
3. Slice off a ½-inch piece of the ginger root.
4. Place a pitcher under the juicer's spout to collect the juice.
5. Feed each ingredient through the juicer's intake tube in the order listed.
6. When the juice stops flowing, remove the pitcher and stir the juice.
7. Serve immediately.

PER SERVING
Calories: 94| Fat: 1g | Protein: 4g | Carbohydrates: 26g | Sugar: 11mg

Celery with Limey Green Extreme
Prep time: 5 minutes | Cook time: 0 minutes | Serves 1

1 cucumber
1 romaine heart
4 celery ribs
1 lime
½ tablespoon wheatgrass powder

1. Wash the cucumber, romaine, celery, and lime.
2. Trim the ends from the cucumber and celery, then cut into 4-inch pieces.
3. Peel the lime and cut into quarters.
4. Place a pitcher under the juicer's spout to collect the juice.
5. Feed the first four ingredients through the juicer's intake tube in the order listed.
6. When the juice stops flowing, remove the pitcher, add the wheatgrass powder, and stir the juice.
7. Serve immediately.

PER SERVING
Calories: 98| Fat: 1g | Protein: 7g | Carbohydrates: 26g | Sugar: 8mg

Chard with Kale Protein Power
Prep time: 5 minutes | Cook time: 0 minutes | Serves 1

1 cup pineapple
5 kale leaves
3 chard leaves
1 cucumber
2 scoops plant-based protein powder

1. Wash the kale, chard, and cucumber.
2. Trim the ends and skin from the pineapple, then remove the core and discard. Cut pineapple into 1-inch chunks.
3. Trim the ends from the cucumber, then cut into 4-inch pieces.
4. Place a pitcher under the juicer's spout to collect the juice.
5. Feed the first four ingredients through the juicer's intake tube in the order listed.
6. When the juice stops flowing, remove the pitcher, add the protein powder, and stir.
7. Serve immediately.

PER SERVING

Calories: 335| Fat: 6g | Protein: 49g | Carbohydrates: 37g | Sugar: 19mg

Gingery Cilantro with Chard Juice
Prep time: 5 minutes | Cook time: 0 minutes | Serves 1

1 cucumber
1 Swiss chard leaf
2 sprigs cilantro
½ small to medium size beet
3 celery ribs
½ lemon
Fresh ginger root

1. Wash all the ingredients.
2. Trim the ends from the cucumber and celery, then cut into 4-inch pieces.
3. Remove any greens from the beet and save for juicing later. Cut the beet into quarters.
4. Peel the lemon and cut into quarters.
5. Slice off a 1-inch piece of the ginger root.
6. Place a pitcher under the juicer's spout to collect the juice.
7. Feed each ingredient through the juicer's intake tube in the order listed.
8. When the juice stops flowing, remove the pitcher and stir the juice.
9. Serve immediately.

PER SERVING

Calories: 76| Fat: 1g | Protein: 4g | Carbohydrates: 22g | Sugar: 10mg

Minty Broccoli Energizing Juice
Prep time: 5 minutes | Cook time: 0 minutes | Serves 1

2 cups broccoli
2 cucumbers
1 green apple
2 mint sprigs

1. Wash all the ingredients.
2. Remove the stalk from the broccoli crown with a knife and discard or save to juice later. Cut the crown into small florets.
3. Trim the ends from the cucumber, then cut into 4-inch pieces.
4. Remove the apple core and discard. Cut the apple into quarters, leaving the peel intact.
5. Place a pitcher under the juicer's spout to collect the juice.
6. Feed each ingredient through the juicer's intake tube in the order listed.
7. When the juice stops flowing, remove the pitcher and stir the juice.
8. Serve immediately.

PER SERVING

Calories: 152| Fat: 1g | Protein: 9g | Carbohydrates: 43g | Sugar: 21mg

Basil with Lemony Herb Juice
Prep time: 5 minutes | Cook time: 0 minutes | Serves 1

2 celery ribs
1 peach
5 basil leaves
2 chard leaves
½ lemon
¼ cup aloe vera juice

1. Wash all the produce.
2. Remove the peach pit and discard. Cut the peach into quarters, leaving the peel intact.
3. Peel the lemon half and cut into quarters.
4. Place a pitcher under the juicer's spout to collect the juice.
5. Feed the first five ingredients through the juicer's intake tube in the order listed.
6. When the juice stops flowing, remove the pitcher, add the aloe vera juice, and stir.
7. Serve immediately.

PER SERVING

Calories: 101| Fat: 1g | Protein: 3g | Carbohydrates: 26g | Sugar: 18mg

Gingered Maca with Cinnamon Juice
Prep time: 5 minutes | Cook time: 0 minutes | Serves 1

1 cup blueberries
2 cups spinach
1 cucumber
Fresh ginger root
½ teaspoon maca powder
¼ teaspoon cinnamon

1. Wash the blueberries, spinach, cucumber, and ginger root.
2. Trim the ends from the cucumber, then cut into 4-inch pieces.
3. Slice off a ½-inch piece of the ginger root.
4. Place a pitcher under the juicer's spout to collect the juice.
5. Feed the first four ingredients through the juicer's intake tube in the order listed.
6. When the juice stops flowing, remove the pitcher, add the maca powder and cinnamon, then stir.
7. Serve immediately.

PER SERVING

Calories: 95| Fat: 1g | Protein: 4g | Carbohydrates: 27g | Sugar: 14mg

Mint with Lemony Kale and Orange
Prep time: 5 minutes | Cook time: 0 minutes | Serves 1

2 oranges
5 carrots
½ lemon
8 kale leaves
15 mint leaves

1. Wash all the ingredients.
2. Peel the oranges and lemon, then cut into quarters.
3. Trim the ends from the carrots, then cut into 4-inch pieces.
4. Place a pitcher under the juicer's spout to collect the juice.
5. Feed each ingredient through the juicer's intake tube in the order listed.
6. When the juice stops flowing, remove the pitcher and stir the juice.
7. Serve immediately.

PER SERVING

Calories: 210| Fat: 3g | Protein: 12g | Carbohydrates: 61g | Sugar: 32mg

Cilantro with Lettuce and Rad Juice
Prep time: 5 minutes | Cook time: 0 minutes | Serves 1

2 cups spinach
1 head leaf lettuce (about 12 leaves)
10 sprigs cilantro
12 carrots
2 radishes
½ lemon

1. Wash all the ingredients.
2. Trim the ends from the carrots, then cut into 4-inch pieces.
3. Remove the tops from radishes.
4. Peel the lemon and cut into quarters.
5. Place a pitcher under the juicer's spout to collect the juice.
6. Feed each ingredient through the juicer's intake tube in the order listed.
7. When the juice stops flowing, remove the pitcher and stir the juice.
8. Serve immediately.

PER SERVING

Calories: 186| Fat: 2g | Protein: 9g | Carbohydrates: 56g | Sugar: 26mg

Lemon with Arugula Power Booster
Prep time: 5 minutes | Cook time: 0 minutes | Serves 2

Handful arugula
½ medium golden or red beet
Handful spinach
3 large carrots
4 cilantro or parsley sprigs
1 small lemon
1 medium red apple

1. Peel, cut, deseed, and/or chop the ingredients as needed.
2. Alternate ingredients, finishing with the apple.
3. Stir the juice and pour into glasses to serve.

PER SERVING

Calories: 112| Fat: 1g | Protein: 2g | Carbohydrates: 28g | Sugar: 17g

Celery Broccoli Power Recharge
Prep time: 5 minutes | Cook time: 0 minutes | Serves 2

Handful arugula
4-inch piece broccoli stalk
4 large carrots
1 orange, peeled
4 large celery stalks

1. Peel, cut, deseed, and/or chop the ingredients as needed.
2. Place a container under the juicer's spout.
3. Alternate ingredients, finishing with the celery.
4. Stir the juice and pour into glasses to serve.

PER SERVING

Calories: 181| Fat: 2g | Protein: 10g | Carbohydrates: 39g | Sugar: 8g

Watermelon with Kale Energy Juice
Prep time: 5 minutes | Cook time: 0 minutes | Serves 2

Handful arugula
2 medium kale leaves
2 large carrots
1 red apple
1 cup watermelon

1. Peel, cut, deseed, and/or chop the ingredients as needed.
2. Place a container under the juicer's spout.
3. Alternate ingredients, finishing with the watermelon.
4. Stir the juice and pour into glasses to serve.

PER SERVING

Calories: 135| Fat: 1g | Protein: 5g | Carbohydrates: 32g | Sugar: 19g

Parsley with Pineapple and Energizing Carrot
Prep time: 5 minutes | Cook time: 0 minutes | Serves 2

2 large carrots
8 parsley sprigs
1 cup pineapple

1. Peel, cut, deseed, and/or chop the ingredients as needed.
2. Place a container under the juicer's spout.
3. Alternate ingredients, finishing with the pineapple.
4. Stir the juice and pour into glasses to serve.

PER SERVING

Calories: 106| Fat: 0g | Protein: 1g | Carbohydrates: 27g | Sugar: 21g

Red Apple Spicy Power Pineapple
Prep time: 5 minutes | Cook time: 0 minutes | Serves 2

Handful arugula
3 large carrots
5 large celery stalks
1-inch piece fresh ginger root
1 cup pineapple
½ cup red apple

1. Peel, cut, deseed, and/or chop the ingredients as needed.
2. Place a container under the juicer's spout.
3. Alternate ingredients, finishing with the apple.
4. Stir the juice and pour into glasses to serve.

PER SERVING

Calories: 284| Fat: 1g | Protein: 4g | Carbohydrates: 70g | Sugar: 53g

Arugula with Zucchini and Cilantro Blend
Prep time: 5 minutes | Cook time: 0 minutes | Serves 2

Handful arugula
4 medium carrots
1 small zucchini
6 cilantro sprigs
6 parsley sprigs
2 small red apples

1. Peel, cut, deseed, and/or chop the ingredients as needed.
2. Place a container under the juicer's spout.
3. Alternate ingredients, finishing with the apple.
4. Stir the juice and pour into glasses to serve.

PER SERVING

Calories: 145| Fat: 0g | Protein: 2g | Carbohydrates: 36g | Sugar: 21g

Arugula And Chard Hydrator
Prep time: 5 minutes | Cook time: 0 minutes | Serves 2

Handful arugula
2 large celery stalks
1 large cucumber
Handful kale
¼ lemon
2 cups Swiss chard
2 small red apples

1. Peel, cut, deseed, and/or chop the ingredients as needed.
2. Place a container under the juicer's spout.
3. Alternate ingredients, finishing with the apple.
4. Stir the juice and pour into glasses to serve.

PER SERVING

Calories: 105| Fat: 1g | Protein: 2g | Carbohydrates: 21g | Sugar: 18g

Spinach with Pineapple and Lemon Boost
Prep time: 5 minutes | Cook time: 0 minutes | Serves 2

Handful arugula
4 small kale leaves
2 cups spinach
½ lemon
1-inch piece fresh ginger root
1 cup pineapple
1 cucumber

1. Peel, cut, deseed, and/or chop the ingredients as needed.
2. 2. Place a container under the juicer's spout.
3. Alternate ingredients, finishing with the cucumber.
4. Stir the juice and pour into glasses to serve.

PER SERVING

Calories: 193| Fat: 0g | Protein: 4g | Carbohydrates: 47g | Sugar: 39g

Chard with Red Pear and Romaine
Prep time: 5 minutes | Cook time: 0 minutes | Serves 2

1 cup red cabbage
2 large Swiss chard leaves
1 firm red pear
4 medium romaine leaves

1. Peel, cut, deseed, and/or chop the ingredients as needed.
2. Place a container under the juicer's spout.
3. Alternate ingredients, finishing with the romaine.
4. Stir the juice and pour into glasses to serve.

PER SERVING

Calories: 125| Fat: 0g | Protein: 2g | Carbohydrates: 30g | Sugar: 18g

Limey Grape-Apple Energy Greens
Prep time: 5 minutes | Cook time: 0 minutes | Serves 2

2 cups black, purple, or red grapes
3 large celery stalks
2 large romaine leaves
Handful spinach
½ lime, peeled
2 small red apples

1. Peel, cut, deseed, and/or chop the ingredients as needed.
2. Place a container under the juicer's spout.
3. Alternate ingredients, finishing with the apple.
4. Stir the juice and pour into glasses to serve.

PER SERVING

Calories: 377| Fat: 1g | Protein: 3g | Carbohydrates: 99g | Sugar: 78g

Berry with Bok Choy Blend
Prep time: 5 minutes | Cook time: 0 minutes | Serves 2

1 cup raspberries
8 medium asparagus spears
1 medium golden or red beet
1 large bok choy stem
4 large romaine leaves
1 large celery stalk

1. Peel, cut, deseed, and/or chop the ingredients as needed.
2. Place a container under the juicer's spout.
3. Alternate ingredients, finishing with the celery.
4. Stir the juice and pour into glasses to serve.

PER SERVING

Calories: 282| Fat: 4g | Protein: 0g | Carbohydrates: 69g | Sugar: 58g

Celery with Red Apple Energy Cocktail
Prep time: 5 minutes | Cook time: 0 minutes | Serves 2

1 cup cauliflower
2 large celery stalks
8 parsley sprigs
2 small red apples
½ cucumber

1. Peel, cut, deseed, and/or chop the ingredients as needed.
2. Place a container under the juicer's spout.
3. Alternate ingredients, finishing with the cucumber.
4. Stir the juice and pour into glasses to serve.

PER SERVING

Calories: 202| Fat: 1g | Protein: 4g | Carbohydrates: 50g | Sugar: 35g

Watermelon with Raspberry Power Juice
Prep time: 5 minutes | Cook time: 0 minutes | Serves 2

4 romaine leaves
1 small red apple
1 orange, peeled
1 cup raspberries
1 cup watermelon
½ cup cucumber

1. Peel, cut, deseed, and/or chop the ingredients as needed.
2. Place a container under the juicer's spout.
3. Feed the first four ingredients one at a time, in the order listed, through the juicer.
4. Stir the juice and pour into glasses to serve.

PER SERVING

Calories: 324| Fat: 1g | Protein: 7g | Carbohydrates: 94g | Sugar: 77g

Romaine with Papaya-Berry Super Cocktail
Prep time: 5 minutes | Cook time: 0 minutes | Serves 2

1 cup papaya
1 cup raspberries
1 cup watermelon
4 large romaine leaves
1 red apple
1 large celery stalk

1. Peel, cut, deseed, and/or chop the ingredients as needed.
2. Place a container under the juicer's spout.
3. Alternate ingredients, finishing with the celery.
4. Stir the juice and pour into glasses to serve.

PER SERVING

Calories: 475| Fat: 1g | Protein: 5g | Carbohydrates: 121g | Sugar: 121g

Red Apple with Raspberry Limeade
Prep time: 5 minutes | Cook time: 0 minutes | Serves 2

1 cup raspberries
2 medium red apples
1 lime, peeled
2 cups watermelon

1. Peel, cut, deseed, and/or chop the ingredients as needed.
2. Place a container under the juicer's spout.
3. Alternate ingredients, finishing with the watermelon.
4. Stir the juice and pour into glasses to serve.

PER SERVING

Calories: 526| Fat: 1g | Protein: 5g | Carbohydrates: 137g | Sugar: 109g

Minty Apple with Tart Refresher
Prep time: 5 minutes | Cook time: 0 minutes | Serves 2

1 red apple
½ large lemon
16 fresh mint leaves
2 cups watermelon

1. Peel, cut, deseed, and/or chop the ingredients as needed.
2. Place a container under the juicer's spout.
3. Alternate ingredients, finishing with the watermelon.
4. Stir the juice and pour into glasses to serve.

PER SERVING

Calories: 192| Fat: 0g | Protein: 2g | Carbohydrates: 50g | Sugar: 39g

Limey Berry and Basil Blend
Prep time: 5 minutes | Cook time: 0 minutes | Serves 2

4 large kale leaves
8 large basil leaves
1 cup blueberries
½ apple
1 small lime, peeled
1 cup watermelon

1. Peel, cut, deseed, and/or chop the ingredients as needed.
2. Place a container under the juicer's spout.
3. Alternate ingredients, finishing with the watermelon.
4. Stir the juice and pour into glasses to serve.

PER SERVING

Calories: 331| Fat: 1g | Protein: 3g | Carbohydrates: 84g | Sugar: 72g.

Coconut Zucchini with Watermelon Limeade
Prep time: 5 minutes | Cook time: 0 minutes | Serves 2

1 medium zucchini
1 lime, peeled
1 cup watermelon
½ cup fresh coconut water

1. Peel, cut, deseed, and/or chop the ingredients as needed.
2. Place a container under the juicer's spout.
3. Alternate ingredients, finishing with the watermelon.
4. Stir the juice and pour into glasses to serve.

PER SERVING

Calories: 82| Fat: 1g | Protein: 2g | Carbohydrates: 20g | Sugar: 13g

Zucchini with Apple Cress Cocktail
Prep time: 5 minutes | Cook time: 0 minutes | Serves 2

4 medium carrots
1 small zucchini
8 parsley sprigs
1 cup watercress
½ lemon
2 small apples

1. Peel, cut, deseed, and/or chop the ingredients as needed.
2. Place a container under the juicer's spout.
3. Alternate ingredients, finishing with the watermelon.
4. Stir the juice and pour into glasses to serve.

PER SERVING

Calories: 135| Fat: 1g | Protein: 2g | Carbohydrates: 35g | Sugar: 22g

Parsley With Grapefruit and Chard
Prep time: 5 minutes | Cook time: 0 minutes | Serves 2

4 medium carrots
2 cups Swiss chard
10 parsley sprigs
1 large pink or red grapefruit, peeled

1. Peel, cut, deseed, and/or chop the ingredients as needed.
2. Place a container under the juicer's spout.
3. Alternate ingredients, finishing with the watermelon.
4. Stir the juice and pour into glasses to serve.

PER SERVING

Calories: 224| Fat: 1g | Protein: 6g | Carbohydrates: 54g | Sugar: 37g

Chard with Kale Energizer

Prep time: 5 minutes | Cook time: 0 minutes | Serves 2

2 large celery stalks
2 cups kale
2 cups Swiss Chard
2 small apples
1 large cucumber

1. Peel, cut, deseed, and/or chop the ingredients as needed.
2. Place a container under the juicer's spout.
3. Alternate ingredients, finishing with the watermelon.
4. Stir the juice and pour into glasses to serve.

PER SERVING

Calories: 112| Fat: 0g | Protein: 3g | Carbohydrates: 27g | Sugar: 18g

Cucumber Kale with Lemon Boost

Prep time: 10 minutes | Cook time: 0 minutes | Serves 3

1 medium golden or red beet
2 large kale leaves
5 parsley sprigs
1 apple
½ lemon
1 large cucumber

1. Peel, cut, deseed, and/or chop the ingredients as needed.
2. Place a container under the juicer's spout.
3. Alternate ingredients, finishing with the watermelon.
4. Stir the juice and pour into glasses to serve.

PER SERVING

Calories: 85 | Fat: 0g | Protein: 1g | Carbohydrates: 21g | Sugar: 14g

Lettuce Hair Rejuvenator

Prep time: 10 minutes | Cook time: 0 minutes | Serves 1

1 handful alfalfa sprouts
4 lettuce leaves
1 lemon
1 cucumber

1. Trim the tops off your carrots and wash all the lettuce leaves and sprouts.
2. Put the sprouts inside the lettuce leaf and juice.

PER SERVING

Calories: 45 | Fat: 1g | Protein: 3g | Carbohydrates: 9g | Sugar: 4g

Carroty Cramp Stopper

Prep time: 5 minutes | Cook time: 0 minutes | Serves 1

2 carrots
6 asparagus spears
6 celery stalks

1. Trim the tops off the carrots and wash your vegetables.

PER SERVING

Calories: 71 | Fat: 0.5g | Protein: 2.3g | Carbohydrates: 16g | Sugar: 7.5g

Garlic with Lemon Anti-Aging Drink

Prep time: 10 minutes | Cook time: 0 minutes | Serves 1

1 garlic clove
2 apples
2 carrots
½ beet
1 lemon

1. Skin the garlic and trim the tops off the carrots.
2. Cut off the top of the beets and peel the lemon.

PER SERVING

Calories: 272 | Fat: 1g | Protein: 3g | Carbohydrates: 70g | Sugar: 48g

Carroty Parsley Jicama Juice

Prep time: 10 minutes | Cook time: 0 minutes | Serves 1

1 slice jicama
3 carrots
½ beet
1 handful parsley

1. Jicama is great for an upset stomach.
2. Make sure you wash all your vegetables and slice the tops of your carrots.

PER SERVING

Calories: 95 | Fat: 0.5g | Protein: 2.4g | Carbohydrates: 22g | Sugar: 12g

Lively Heart Juice

Prep time: 5 minutes | Cook time: 0 minutes | Serves 1

3 apples
½ beet

1. Wash all your vegetables. Peel the apple if it is not organic.
2. Cut the top of the beet and let the juicing begin.

PER SERVING

Calories: 302 | Fat: 1g | Protein: 2g | Carbohydrates: 79g | Sugar: 60g

Veggie Bone and Nail Health Juice
Prep time: 5 minutes | Cook time: 0 minutes | Serves 1

½ cucumber
2 kale leaves
½ green bell pepper
1 lemon

1. Wash and trim your vegetables.
2. Make sure you peel the lemon and cucumber if they are not organic.

PER SERVING

Calories: 39 | Fat: 0.4g | Protein: 2g | Carbohydrates: 9g | Sugar: 4g

Carroty Stamina Booster
Prep time: 5 minutes | Cook time: 0 minutes | Serves 1

½ cucumber
2 bundles Bok choy
4 carrots

1. Trim the tops off the carrots and peel your cucumber if it is not organic.

PER SERVING

Calories: 112 | Fat: 0.8g | Protein: 3g | Carbohydrates: 26g | Sugar: 13g

Lettuce with Pancreas Pump
Prep time: 10 minutes | Cook time: 0 minutes | Serves 1

2 apples
4 carrots
2 lettuce leaves
4 string beans
2 Brussels sprouts
1 handful sprouts

1. Make sure you wash all your vegetables.
2. Put the sprouts inside the lettuce leaf and juice.

PER SERVING

Calories: 321 | Fat: 1.4g | Protein: 6g | Carbohydrates: 80g | Sugar: 51g

Apple Cranberry Anti-Aging Juice
Prep time: 5 minutes | Cook time: 0 minutes | Serves 1

3 apples
1 cup cranberries

1. Cut the seeds out of the apple (use organic apples only).
2. Put the rest of the fruit in the juicer.

PER SERVING

Calories: 421 | Fat: 1.2g | Protein: 1.4g | Carbohydrates: 110g | Sugar: 87g

Gingery Holistic Blast
Prep time: 10 minutes | Cook time: 0 minutes | Serves 1

3 apples
2 bunches grapes
1 tiny piece ginger
1 lemon

1. Peel the lemon and apples if they are not organic and get rid of the grape stems if not organic. Wash well.
2. Pass through the juicer

PER SERVING

Calories: 303 | Fat: 1g | Protein: 2g | Carbohydrates: 81g | Sugar: 59g

Happy Day Juice
Prep time: 10 minutes | Cook time: 0 minutes | Serves 1

1 cup cranberries
1 bunch green grapes, preferably organic, with stems
1 (1-inch) pineapple round

1. If the grapes are not organic, remove the stems. If the pineapple is not organic, same deal; remove the rind.
2. Pass through the juicer

PER SERVING

Calories: 593 | Fat: 1.4g | Protein: 5g | Carbohydrates: 156g | Sugar: 120g

Lemon and Cucumber Brain Juice
Prep time: 10 minutes | Cook time: 0 minutes | Serves 1

1 broccoli shoot and floret, diced
1 cucumber
1 lemon
½ carrot

1. Dice the broccoli up so that it fits in the juicer.
2. Peel the lemon if it is not organic.
3. Pass through your juicer

PER SERVING

Calories: 77 | Fat: 1g | Protein: 4g | Carbohydrates: 16g | Sugar: 7g

Juicy Liver Life
Prep time: 10 minutes | Cook time: 0 minutes | Serves 1

½ beet, with greens
3 apples

1. Wash all thoroughly, remove apple stems, and put the beet in.
2. Pass through the juicer

PER SERVING

Calories: 302 | Fat: 1g | Protein: 2g | Carbohydrates: 79g | Sugar: 60g

Celery Wrinkle Reducer juice

Prep time: 10 minutes | Cook time: 0 minutes | Serves 1

1 cucumber, with skin and cut into pieces
2 carrots, peeled and cut into pieces
1 celery stalk
2 apples, unpeeled and cut into pieces

1. Clean the cucumber, carrots, and apples. Extract the juice from them in the juicer and add a lot of water to it.
2. Add the celery stalk. In a slender glass put some freshly chopped pieces of green apples. Strain the juice and put it into the glass.
3. Serve it cold or at room temperature. This will enable you to get rid of wrinkles without hassle.
4. Enjoy!

PER SERVING

Calories: 269 | Fat: 1g | Protein: 4g | Carbohydrates: 69g | Sugar: 46g

Minty Memory Booster Juice

Prep time: 10 minutes | Cook time: 0 minutes | Serves 1

1 cucumber
1 carrot
1 green apple
¼ cup parsley
¼ cup mint
1 celery stalk
½-inch piece fresh ginger
½ lemon, peeled

1. Wash and peel all your non-organic vegetables.
2. Cut up to fit in the juicer and enjoy.

PER SERVING

Calories: 203 | Fat: 2g | Protein: 3g | Carbohydrates: 47g | Sugar: 33g

Appendix 1 Measurement Conversion Chart

Volume Equivalents (Dry)	
US STANDARD	METRIC (APPROXIMATE)
1/8 teaspoon	0.5 mL
1/4 teaspoon	1 mL
1/2 teaspoon	2 mL
3/4 teaspoon	4 mL
1 teaspoon	5 mL
1 tablespoon	15 mL
1/4 cup	59 mL
1/2 cup	118 mL
3/4 cup	177 mL
1 cup	235 mL
2 cups	475 mL
3 cups	700 mL
4 cups	1 L

Weight Equivalents	
US STANDARD	METRIC (APPROXIMATE)
1 ounce	28 g
2 ounces	57 g
5 ounces	142 g
10 ounces	284 g
15 ounces	425 g
16 ounces (1 pound)	455 g
1.5 pounds	680 g
2 pounds	907 g

Volume Equivalents (Liquid)		
US STANDARD	US STANDARD (OUNCES)	METRIC (APPROXIMATE)
2 tablespoons	1 fl.oz.	30 mL
1/4 cup	2 fl.oz.	60 mL
1/2 cup	4 fl.oz.	120 mL
1 cup	8 fl.oz.	240 mL
1 1/2 cup	12 fl.oz.	355 mL
2 cups or 1 pint	16 fl.oz.	475 mL
4 cups or 1 quart	32 fl.oz.	1 L
1 gallon	128 fl.oz.	4 L

Temperatures Equivalents	
FAHRENHEIT(F)	CELSIUS(C) APPROXIMATE
225 °F	107 °C
250 °F	120 ° °C
275 °F	135 °C
300 °F	150 °C
325 °F	160 °C
350 °F	180 °C
375 °F	190 °C
400 °F	205 °C
425 °F	220 °C
450 °F	235 °C
475 °F	245 °C
500 °F	260 °C

Appendix 2 Index

DAWN J. WASHINGTON

Made in United States
Troutdale, OR
06/26/2025

32309545R00066